T0338091

Miguel Abensour

Utopia from Thomas More to Walter Benjamin

Translated by
Raymond N. MacKenzie

L'Utopie de Thomas More à Walter Benjamin
by Miguel Abensour
©2000 1st edition, 2009, Sens&Tonka éditeurs

This edition published by Univocal Publishing
as
Utopia from Thomas More to Walter Benjamin
by Miguel Abensour
Translated by Raymond N. MacKenzie, 2017

© Univocal, January 2017
411 N. Washington Ave, Suite 10
Minneapolis, MN 55401

A special thank you to Hubert Tonka and Miguel Abensour.

Cover design by Jason Wagner
Distributed by the University of Minnesota Press

ISBN 9781945414008
Library of Congress Control Number 2016953432

Table of Contents

Note on the Translation

This translation of Miguel Abensour's *Utopia from Thomas More to Walter Benjamin* needs a word of explanation regarding Abensour's quotations from other scholars. Due to the high number of such quotations, many of which were translations (into French) themselves, the translator and publisher agreed to take a somewhat unusual approach: instead of seeking out English translations where they exist, we decided to translate directly from the texts that Abensour himself used. Of course, many of these works—beginning with More's *Utopia* itself—do exist in excellent English translations, but those differ, sometimes significantly, from the French versions that the author used. In some cases, notably with the Walter Benjamin material, the French versions include references to material that is not included in the English translations. Thus, in an attempt to remain faithful to the author's text, we translated the quotations anew. The reader will find that a work is cited in English in the text, but the footnotes refer to the French version: thus, for example, the text will refer to More's book as *Utopia*, while the footnote lists it as *L'Utopie*. The result is, we believe, a more faithful representation of Miguel Abensour's book and thought.

Avant-Propos

Thomas More and Walter Benjamin?

Bringing these two names together into an unexpected constellation is surprising enough. They have little in common, apart from one essential thing: utopia. But the point here is not to discover some unknown filiation between the two, nor to write a history of utopia with Thomas More as the starting point and Walter Benjamin as the destination. While it is true that Thomas More is indeed the inventor, with his Utopia, *of a new rhetorical device, one with which he attempts an original intervention in the political arena, Walter Benjamin by no means represents the completion of the utopic tradition which, under diverse forms, has continued to manifest itself after him. Rather, the project is one of seizing hold of utopia in two different but powerful moments in its fortunes: the first moment is that of utopia's beginning, and the second is the moment when utopia faced its greatest danger, the moment that Walter Benjamin called "catastrophe."*

Let us also be careful to note that the two works are not similarly motivated; the one invents a form, a new kind of discourse at the margins of political philosophy, for which it creates the name "utopia," born under the sign of scholarly ambiguity, while the other, more reflexive, more critical, seeks out the conditions for a new interpretation of utopia, on an order more political than historical, in order to provoke an eventual reactivation of it. In the face of the catastrophe—the texts of Walter Benjamin as well as his correspondence with Adorno stretch from 1935 to 1939—under what conditions was it possible to create some living relationship with utopia, to invoke utopia, to transform it in such a way as to make it a weapon against the hand of death darkening Europe in those years? During his Parisian exile, toward the end of October 1935, Walter Benjamin sounded the depths of the abyss opening around him, describing his work as a sentinel or witness thus:

"In any case, I have not at all been inclined to make sense of the world as it is today. On this planet, many cultures have already drowned in blood and horror. So naturally we must hope that one day the planet will know one that has freed itself from blood and horror—and in fact, just like Scheerbart, I am inclined to believe that the planet is awaiting such a thing. But that we will be able to present the world with such a gift to celebrate her one hundred

millionth or four hundred millionth birthday: that is terribly doubtful. And if we cannot, as punishment for the good wishes we have blindly expressed, she will ultimately present us with her final judgment.

"As for what immediately concerns me, I am trying to aim my telescope through the bloodied mist at a mirage from the nineteenth century, which I shall try to describe the way it will look to a future world, one liberated from magic."[1]

Thus the tonality is not the same: Thomas More's is one of morning gaiety, letting himself appear to be playing with ideas, and taking delight in writing, in opposition to the miseries of the era, a kind of "golden handbook" to charm both readers and those who want to put it into practice; Walter Benjamin's tone is an exercise in suspicion, worsened by the controversy with Adorno, but far from being confined or immobilized within that sad disposition, and it asks the question: how do we preserve the very thing that taught us about salvation, or in short, how do we liberate utopia from both magic and myth?

Utopia poses a question. Not simply in the sense of a problem to be resolved and at the same time eliminated, the way many tried to do with "the Jewish question," but in the sense that, within the economy of the human condition, utopia, the aim of social alterity—of all social otherness— is ceaselessly being reborn, coming back to life despite all the blows rained down upon it, as if human resistance had taken up its residence within it. The permanence of utopia poses a question. Apart from the surrealist intervention, with its rehabilitation of the poetic imaginary, two thoughts, each opening a different pathway, can help us in coming to terms with the idea.

According to Ernst Bloch, the persistence of utopia across the centuries arises out of an ontological locus, of Being considered as both in process and incomplete. And it would be in fact from within the incompleteness of Being—within the not-yet—that utopia finds its inextinguishable source, its most certain principle, as if the utopian impulse came to life borne upon, somehow supported by this ontological tension and gave itself the task of completing Being, through aiming at its own goals of Surplus and of the Essential. "The Not, qua the Not-Yet," writes Ernst Bloch, "traverses Being-become [l'Être devenu] … The Not in the sense of the Not-Yet-in-Process thus makes utopia the real state of incompleteness, of the always fragmentary essence within all objects."[2] *Being escapes, not in the sense of Being as such but simply in the sense of incomplete Being. And thus, to continue with Ernst Bloch, it would seem that the full accomplishment of*

1.
Walter Benjamin to Werner Kraft, 28 October 1935, in *Correspondance 1929-1940*, trans. Guy Petitdemange (Paris: Aubier-Montaigne, 1979), 195. In Benjamin's thought, Paul Scheerbart played a utopian role similar to that of Fourier.

2.
Ernst Bloch, *Le Principe espérance*, trans. Françoise Wuilmart, vol. I (Paris: Gallimard, 1976), 371.

Being will coincide with the true end of utopia. He explains, "This is only if a Being similar to utopia … seizes the activating content of the hic et nunc, *the fundamental sentiment of this agitating drive: hope itself will also be absorbed entirely into the completed reality."[3] This hypothesis is certainly conceivable, but beneath its amiable surface it teems with formidable illusions involving the full coincidence of self with self. While awaiting the return to self, or remaining in the "foyer," utopia resists and perseveres.*

For his part, Emmanuel Levinas—who, we know, has called the fundamental character of ontology into question, to the point of seeking out, in the course of his appreciative reading of Ernst Bloch, another text beneath the ontological one, as if the latter had been a kind of superimposition— locates the source of utopia elsewhere, within that enigmatic region that is the human, within the region of relations between people, that "under-researched field." Levinas refers to "the utopian human" in his preface to the work of Martin Buber, Utopia and Socialism.[4] *Emmanuel Levinas invites us to think utopia under the aegis of the encounter, of the relation to the other as such, in his or her incomparable uniqueness. Thus he removes utopia from the order of knowing, and its effects from the order of power, so as to assign it to the order of the social or, better, to that of proximity, so that it may reveal what it really is, a thought, a form of thinking "other than knowing." While being careful to avoid being duped by the moral, Emmanuel Levinas explores the byways of utopia by means of what he calls the ethical fact: "The relation in which the I encounters the Thou is the ground and origin of the advent of ethics."[5] This is why Levinas attempts to dissipate the ambiguity, as he sees it, in the thought of Ernst Bloch who, beginning with the distinction between Being and Man, situates utopia in both the field of ontology and that of ethics at the same time. This critical approach results in a new complexity for utopia, turning it toward a different destination: no longer toward an accord between Being and Man in the name of the Essential from which essence issues, but instead toward the manifestation of the human as proceeding from Being* qua *Being, beyond essence. Thus the emergence of the human from Being, no longer in the form of a conquest of self or place of origin, but instead from the discovery of the no-place (*u-topos*) that doubles and haunts every place.*

Going outward to the other—is this really a going outward? So asks Emmanuel Levinas. For this "nothing outside of man," to use the poet Paul Celan's phrase, this suspension of essence, this halting of the conatus *returns us "to the excentric sphere that leads to the human."[6] This would be the creation of a new utopian level, one that would manifest itself beyond*

3. Ibid., 228.

4. Emmanuel Levinas, preface to *Utopie et socialisme,* by Martin Buber (Paris: Aubier-Montaigne, 1977), 10.

5. Emmanuel Levinas, *De Dieu qui vient à l'idée* (Paris: Vrin, 1982), 225.

6. Emmanuel Levinas, "De l'Être à l'Autre," in *Noms propres* (Montpellier: Fata Morgana, 1976), 63.

7.
Levinas,
De Dieu qui
vient à l'idée,
25-26.

8.
Levinas,
"De l'Être à l'
Autre," 63. For
more on Levi-
nas's specific
conception
of ethical
dimensions
of "escaping
oneself and
going outward
toward the
other man,"
see his work,
De l'évasion
(Saint-Clé-
ment-de-
Rivière: Fata
Morgana,
1982) [*On*
Escape, trans.
Bettina Bergo
(Stanford, CA:
Stanford
University
Press, 2003)]

ideologies in the creation of an opening toward social alterity. Levinas asks, "The invisible face of this ontological interruption, of this époché—*would it not coincide with the movement toward a better society?"[7] To explain this "new utopian level" belonging to the sphere of the human, Levinas suggests a hypothesis: "It is as if the human were a type that permitted an absolute rupture within its inner, logical space, its extension, as if in going outward toward the other man one transcended the human, toward utopia."[8] Utopia, far from being presented as a kind of dream of an emptiness with no location, or as "a fated, accursed wandering" in an evil infinity, instead is conceived as the clarity of a man revealing himself, for indeed the clarity of utopia is necessary for a man to reveal himself outside of the darkness in which he struggles—the darkness of the "there is," the darkness of the neutral. To the light of the intelligible, to the light of ontology, the poet, sustained by the philosopher, opposes the clarity of utopia.*

The opposition man/Being, that "remarkable intellectual gesture" in Levinas's words, thus opens up an alternative for thinking the resistance of utopia, whether this latter is nourished in the home of incomplete Being, or whether it is born and reborn out of the human itself. But what does all this matter compared to the hatred of utopia, that sad passion eternally reasserted over and over, that repetitive symptom which, generation after generation, afflicts the defenders of the existing order, seized with their fear of alterity? Instead of wearing ourselves out refuting that disposition yet again—hatred is deaf, hatred is blind—let us simply suggest to the sworn enemies of utopia, that a society without utopia, one deprived of utopia, is precisely a totalitarian society, caught up in the illusion of completion, of thinking it has realized utopia. It is in this sense that the theory of Ernst Bloch may be considered dangerous, despite the firm distinction it draws between utopia and ideology. The distance in terms of difference is not impossible to traverse, and this is not a matter of wandering but rather an indication that no human society can avoid being in relation to a better society, to the idea of a better society, as if the social in its manifestation were interrogating itself, and were irresistibly being worked upon by a "better," by aspiring toward a "better," as if there were a utopia whose origins lay in the social.

If we concede the persistence of utopia, by one or another path, it may be of some interest to return to its birth, with Thomas More; no utopian idea or practice can do without connecting to its initium, *nor can it do without taking note of the complex relationship—critical and* redemptive—that Walter Benjamin, much closer to our time, established between utopia and "catastrophe."

Two unequivocal positions appear untenable with regard to utopia: its systematic depreciation as well as its uncritical exaltation. Neither wishes to see what utopia was in its beginnings, nor how some, though facing extreme peril, will work to save it from the inner threats that would destroy it. It may therefore be fruitful to allow the lessons of Thomas More to cross paths with those of Walter Benjamin. In the face of disaster, the most immediate reaction is to turn away from utopia, to set it aside and wait for better times, to "hedge our bets," in order to put up a better fight, defending and saving what is closest to us—or at least what can be saved. The power of Walter Benjamin lay in his ability to see the impasse this spontaneous reaction leads to; in the presence of extreme peril, utopia seemed to him more than ever to be the order of the day. In a time of crisis, the need for rescue seemed infinitely greater, and to respond to that need, it seemed best to first rescue utopia by forcing it free from myth and transforming it into a "dialectical image." It seemed best to turn himself toward the distant future in order to rescue what was closest and most familiar. And in fact Benjamin was not the only one to react in this way. Consider the journal of Etty Hillesum, Une Vie bouleversée. A young Dutch Jew, who, even when standing at the gates of hell—she died in Auschwitz in 1943—thought it was essential and vital to retain, if not an image of happiness, at least the idea of "an enlarged horizon." "I maintain," she wrote, "that if we cannot oppose this gloom with some powerful ray of light that will stand as the promise of beginning over again on entirely new grounds, we will be lost, lost for good, lost forever."[9] And even after the Shoah, when it seemed that no utopia could possibly survive such an event, at that very point of rupture, Emmanuel Levinas issued a denial to the deniers. The philosopher wrote, to anyone surprised to find a work centered on the Good and the relationship with the Other in the aftermath of that war: "The idea that the human finds its meaning in the relationship of a person with an other—is this optimistic, or is it pessimistic? It certainly may seem to be an ironic idea, coming just after the horrors of 1933-1945. Perhaps it is utopian. But that term does not frighten me. I think, in fact, that the human, as such, can only awaken in 'man as he is' . . . Putting my place and time into question, and into being, is this not utopian? But to retrieve the human, not from where it founders within the real and effects the political history of the world, but from within the ruptures in that history, in the crises—to do this is not to assert that the human is nothing...."[10] And so it is that we can understand

9.
Etty Hillesum,
Une Vie bouleversée: Journal, 1941-1943 (Paris: Seuil, 1985), 182.

10.
Emmanuel Levinas, interview with Salomon Malka, in *Lire Levinas* (Paris: Cerf, 1989), 109-110.

why, right up until his final days, Walter Benjamin kept the utopian writings of Charles Fourier close by.

This approach, complex and surprising in some ways as it is: is it really so far removed from that of Thomas More? Was it not already there when he created it—Utopia—that is, at the very time when he was anxious to rescue, in the face of a world in transformation, the imperative of justice, opening up an unknown path for it, a path other than that of millenarian Christianity? In any case, without forcing the argument, one can discern certain "connections" concerning utopia between Thomas More and Walter Benjamin. The sign of ambiguity arises with both, that intellectual ambiguity found in the very name of utopia for Thomas More, and arising out of a dangerous intricacy that Walter Benjamin locates in the myth. Disentangling utopia from the myth: would this not be an attempt to dissolve its ambiguity in order to give it back its emancipatory potentialities? Both associate utopia with the ruse, present under various faces in the work of Thomas More, and linked to the struggle to break free of the dream and become awakened for the author of The Arcades Project. "Awakening," writes Walter Benjamin, "requires the ruse. It is through ruse, and not without it, that we can pull ourselves up out of the dream."[11]

11.
Walter
Benjamin,
Paris, capitale du XIXe siècle
(Paris: Cerf, 1989), 893.

But above all, both aim, while following their different paths, at forging a strange relation to utopia, one marked by both proximity and distance or displacement at the same time, as if utopia were an attitude, a disposition, a way of thinking, or even a spiritual exercise to which one can only be fully committed by keeping an irreducible distance. The signs of all this are multiple: the smile of Fourier, or the "innovation technique" of William Morris in News from Nowhere which, while placing the inherited story of utopia within the romance genre, at the same time deconstructs it by putting it to the proof, by exposing to experimentation that which had classically been presented as a solution. In the present case, the oblique path—Thomas More's—and the way of the sentry—Walter Benjamin's—reveal this distance in their different ways. And we could even consider Thomas More as having set himself up as an observer of his own text in writing Utopia, as if that redemptive critique had impregnated utopia from its very first written form. For in both cases it is a matter of disturbing readers, teaching us to resist the very charm of utopia and its enchantments, inviting us to invent for ourselves, through utopia, another form of relationship to that which is different, forever exhorting us to resist the thrall of the always dangerous myth. Thus, even if utopia is a close relative of "mental heroics," it is also related to *patience, to approaches that proceed by twists and turns rather than burst out of the fires of enthusiasm . . . Utopia? An exercise in heroic patience.*

Certainly, emancipation returns upon itself; certainly, emancipation follows the example of reason, and knows the dialectic of emancipation, that is to say, according to the first critical theory (Adorno, Horkheimer), that paradoxical movement by which modern liberty turns into its contrary, giving birth to new forms of domination and oppression—to barbarism even—despite the liberatory intentions it begins with. But this event, far from liquidating emancipation, and utopia along with it (as some, postmoderns or otherwise, try to delude us into thinking, forgetful of critical theory, and inviting us to abandon the very idea of emancipation)—this event opens up a new path toward utopia. Among its tasks are pointing out the blind spots in modern emancipation, those loci of mythologization which leave it wide open to turning into its opposite—to surround them so as to submit them to critique and to "absolute distance," to use Fourier's term. In short, to open up and map out new "lines of flight" for utopia, toward a new no-place.

By invoking these two names, Thomas More and Walter Benjamin, other names must come forward—Joseph Déjacque, William Morris, André Breton, author of the Ode to Charles Fourier. *A bridge must be built linking the "spirit of utopia" and what we shall call, in order to denote the persistence of utopia despite its oft-pronounced deaths, "the new spirit of utopia."*

Thomas More, or, the Oblique Path

Do our contemporaries know how to read utopias, and specifically the foundational work, that of Thomas More?[12] The question may appear disrespectful, not to say overbold, but it must be posed, given the anti-utopian literature that, with scarcely any trial, has condemned *Utopia* to a place in the genealogy of totalitarianism.

Those who are so prompt to denounce tyranny—and for that, one can only rejoice—sometimes practice a style of reading that is not only "barbarous" but precisely tyrannical, following the example of the tyrant who denounced Plato in his Letter VII. The latter, after his third sojourn in Syracuse, wanted to assure himself that philosophy had genuinely inflamed the heart of Dionysius. Now he reported, horrified, that the tyrant had forged a kind of "platonism" made up of misunderstood ideas. "Now, as a result, I understand that Dionysius has composed his own text out of things that he thought I said, a product of his own mind, without any of the things in it that he had heard."[13] Contesting the legitimacy of this operation, which arose out of a confusion of the philosopher's actions with his philosophical sayings, Plato, thinking back on his teaching, says that "it is not a matter, as it is in other fields, of things which can be formulated in propositions."[14]

The allusion to Letter VII has a direct bearing on *Utopia*, in that recalling it may serve to militate against grossly inadequate methods of reading. And moreover, it allows us to define the region of thought to which utopia belongs: The very complex relationship between the tyrant and the philosopher, that volatile mixture of attraction and rivalry, of petition and of threat that appears already in the dialogue on counsel in Book I of *Utopia*—the differential relation between *Utopia* and Plato's *Republic*: at last the question arises concerning the philosopher in particular circumstances and the communication of philosophy, that is, the question of giving counsel to a

12.
The edition used here is Thomas More, *L'Utopie*, ed. Marie Delcourt (Brussels: Renaissance du livre, n.d.). This edition lacks the paratexts More used; those are cited from the excellent bilingual edition of André Prévost (Paris: Mame, 1978).

13.
Plato, Letter VII, in *Oeuvres complètes* II (Paris: Gallimard, [Bibliothèque de la Pléiade], 1950), 1208.

14.
Ibid., 341c.

prince. The prosecutors of *Utopia*, in such a hurry to conclude, drew attention to the prudence of Plato, who knew the constraints that always accompany petitions to tyrants, and that in order to make oneself heard by them, one had to have recourse to indirect methods. And thus in Letter VII Plato details the precautions that the philosopher who wants to communicate with a tyrant must take, so as to avoid putting his own life in danger: "Certainly, we did not speak openly, for our own safety would have been compromised; but we cloaked our words, striving with all our powers to communicate to him that everyone, for his own safety and that of his subjects, must proceed this way, and that to proceed in another way would lead to the contrary for everyone concerned."[15]

15.
Ibid., 332 d-e.

If the *Utopia* of Thomas More shares in the modern idea of method, it nonetheless establishes connections with the tradition of political philosophy, such that it can elaborate in an unexpected way the relationship between writing and prudence. Let us state at the outset that the question of tyranny—whether that of the prince or that of opinion—or the question of a tyrannical reading is inscribed at the very heart of the invention of *Utopia*, or, rather, of the invention of the indirect writing that constitutes *Utopia*.

Everything takes place as if modern criticism as a whole, every bit as impatient as the tyrant of Syracuse, perceived *Utopia* as a social project, like a constitutional proposition, or like a model, in short. Now, in its very texture—inasmuch as one consents to follow the arcane pathways Thomas More lays out—*Utopia* ceaselessly works to persuade the reader that this thing, this "truly golden handbook," is neither a kind of plan nor any kind of model. Thus a mistake arises at the very beginning: criticism hurls itself against those theses or doctrinal propositions that it wants to extract from the book—whether it be social Christianity, or socio-economic planning, or communism—without taking the trouble to see that *Utopia* is the fruit of an extraordinarily complex textual apparatus, full of traps, one that toys with the reader's desire, always exposing it as an illusion; it is intellectual play, subtle and erudite, the acrobatic play of the humanist, simple as a dove but cunning as a serpent; so that when, given all that, one pretends to understand Thomas More better than he understood himself, one is set up for mockery as a conceited fool.

And thus any reading that does not take this elaborate textual machine into account, this huntsman's art, this veritable "exercise in patience," is immediately condemned to fall well short of *Utopia*, whether that reading attempts to damn or to praise the book, if it fails to consent to following the many detours of the book and its oblique approach.

The Crisis of Interpretation

From out of this fundamental misunderstanding arises the crisis of interpretation and the aporias of criticism where we find a constant oscillation between two types of reading, one realist and the other allegorical.

Realist readings can be divided into two camps, the Catholics on the one hand and the socialists or communists on the other. Two traditions thus battle over the author of *Utopia*. The Soviets reserved a place for Thomas More in their revolutionary pantheon, and his name is inscribed on a plaque in Red Square in Moscow. The Catholics beatified More in 1886, and canonized him as a saint in 1935. But apart from their differences, the realist readings have a quality in common: they both insist on the political dimension of the book—the title page proclaims *De optimo Rei publicae statu*, or "on the best state of a commonwealth"— but both remain in total ignorance of the question of writing that the book raises. Their perspective reduces *Utopia* to a political program, to a model for society.

Thus Karl Kautsky, in *Thomas More and His Utopia* (1888), presents More as a remarkable precursor of modern socialism. Though the author of *Utopia* was a child of his era and thus reproduced in himself its limitations, its humanism, its practical knowledge of law and economics, the birth of merchant capitalism taking place around him—all this would have permitted him not only to critique the new mode of production, but to paint in broad outlines a superior mode, one destined to supplant capitalism. Conforming to the logic of a historicist reading, *Utopia* itself is seen as issuing from the will to find a fantastic solution to the contradictions that this era still languishing in its immaturity was not yet ready to otherwise resolve. In this sense, Thomas More would be the true father of "utopian socialism," a phrase here denoting an inadequate approach—the enlightened despotism of King Utopus—and not the real goal.

For R. W. Chambers, a Roman Catholic critic and author of *Thomas More* (1935), the socialist reading of *Utopia* is quite simply a historical error and an offensive appropriation. Far from prophesying modern communism, Thomas More was instead the defender of a society in decline, and one who wished to restore the values of medieval Christian solidarity. He was not depicting an ideal State, but rather presenting a virtuous pagan city with the intent of arousing a sense of shame among Christian readers who had failed to progress even to the perfection of a city founded on human reason alone.

Thomas More, working under the influence of a desire to restore, set himself in opposition to the modern world: and hence his opposition to the new State and the new art of governing—that is, Machiavellianism—and his opposition to the new merchant economy. But more precisely, in the midst of that conflict between nascent capitalism and communitarian Christian values, Thomas More opted for a reactionary method designed to return to the communal ideal such as it had been practiced under medieval monarchy. And thus the model that *Utopia* proposes is based on that of the Benedictine monastery, with its discipline and its authority standing in opposition to modern liberty. Curiously, Chambers, who is so anxious to put More back in his own time, remains silent with regard to the rhetorical controversies that the author of *Utopia* participated in, and neglects the question of the art of writing, which was so very important for Thomas More and his contemporaries, whether Erasmus or Machiavelli.[16]

It is worth noting that there is no necessary connection between the Catholic and the realist interpretations.

16.
R. W.
Chambers,
Thomas More
(London:
Harcourt
Brace, 1935).

André Prévost, a Catholic critic and the editor of a remarkable bilingual (Latin and French) edition of *Utopia*, presents a consistently allegorical reading. What we call allegorical readings are those that foreground the question of writing in *Utopia*, that approach *Utopia* as writing but which, on the other hand, by this same approach efface the political question, that of the search for a better government, transforming it into a spiritual quest. Prévost's is a truly allegorical reading because it seeks to unmask a moral interpretation beneath the literal, historical-political layers. From this perspective, the writing itself receives the greatest attention: the textual devices, the utopian vocabulary, the author's comic or ironic turns—all these figure as so many narrow gates through which meaning might pass, leading the reader toward an ascent upward, from the historical sense to the spiritual one. André Prévost, invoking the distinction between story and discourse, and exploring the conflict between these two dimensions of the text, denounces those interpretations that "hypostatize" the Utopian institutions, giving the city More described an objective existence and endowing it with the value of a kind of model.[17] "For More," he argues, "*Utopia* is essentially an organ for discovery, a sort of heuristic. To see in it an objective model on which to construct a society and a politics is an error."[18] This is the crazy principle, says the editor of *Utopia*, that has historically dominated interpretations of the book. Appearing as the mirror of a well-ordered political community, *Utopia*, via its internal movements, via its own maieutics, calls for us to "shatter the mirror," thus opening up the transcendent dimension of the "interior Utopia." Prévost writes, "The dialectic of the message brings us to a catharsis, the moment when, by refusing to commit to a concrete model whose limits one must deny along with its caducity, the spirit ascends to the Elsewhere, to the transcendent Utopia."[19] In short, it is less a matter of annulling the text than one of sublimating it and submitting oneself to an initiatory experience that engenders a metanoia, a complete reversal of the interior life. He continues, "Once more, More's construct is revealed as, not a paradigmatic example to be imitated in a literal

17. André Prévost, *L'Utopie de Thomas More* (Paris: Mame, 1978), cxxiii.

18. Ibid., cxv.

19. Ibid., cxxv, n3.

manner, but as an instrument for an inner rebirth. Its dialectical movement leads not to reforms or revolutions but to conversion, to a return, to a communion with others via a common nature, to the acceptance of the fundamental principles that bring to the fore our responsibility before God."[20]

Prévost's concern for the writing itself is very valuable, and it brings much light to the text, but the position he takes—the rejection of the political dimension—is not tenable without difficulty. Criticism must be constrained by ultimately consenting to that return, that "ascent" from the political under the guise of a micro-utopia, again resembling the monastery, though made more modest by being located within the human struggle for a transcendent utopia, destined to caducity and bearing witness to human finitude.

But are we irremediably condemned to this less-than-satisfying alternative: either entertain the political question while denying the written-ness of the book, or focusing on the written quality but at the price—and what a price!—of effacing the political dimension? Should we not rather try to think the question of writing along with the question of politics? Instead of dissociating the two, we should rather cross the two so as to short-circuit the constraints of both realist and allegorical readings.

To do so is to recognize that the invention of utopian writing opens up a singular intervention within the field of politics; it is to admit that the political project, the search for a better government, requires recourse to a new form of writing. *Utopia* will be political, but not through what it says—its propositions, its theses, its themes—but rather, through the effectuation of the text.

In order to make our way down this path, we must return to the great discovery of Leo Strauss, in his *Persecution and the Art of Writing*, regarding a forgotten art of writing. It will follow that *Utopia* has the status of a political work, but for all that it is no model; it would seem that the writing of Thomas More is allegorical, but in a new sense, without necessarily entailing any depreciation of the political leading to a spiritual conversion. Will *Utopia* then be in fact the complication of the political?

20.
Ibid.,
cxxviii.

To follow Raphael Hythloday on his sea journey, or rather the narrative of his journey, his "odyssey," it would be wise to first equip ourselves with the compass provided by Leo Strauss.

Let us briefly review the main ideas of the latter. The condemnation of Socrates—for while introducing a new mode into the city, he showed imprudence—draws attention to the phenomenon of persecution, which threatens philosophical inquiry in every human city. How can one communicate an independent thought, one capable of overthrowing some orthodoxy in a given society, without coming to the tragic end that Socrates did? The proper path of philosophy is to open up a passage from those opinions that have taken root in a city, and that have worked to reproduce the city exactly as it is, and to move toward the knowledge of "all things," a knowledge that may well overturn the political order by calling into question certain things that do not fit with received opinion; in short, the work of philosophy is to replace opinion with knowledge. The nature of philosophy is to do harm to what Leo Strauss called "the social element," to its tissue—that is, opinion. "Philosophy or science," he writes, "is thus the attempt to dissolve the very element that society breathes, and thus it poses a danger to society."[21] If philosophy chooses to respect the opinions of a given society, it still cannot consider them as true. The hallmark of free thought is to have no need of anything outside itself, and it cannot tolerate external limitations. How can one satisfy these requirements of independent thought without risking persecution?

From Jewish-Arab philosophical works of the medieval period, Leo Strauss rediscovered a particular method of writing, that is, writing "between the lines." This secret art of writing allows free thought to devote itself to the search for truth without openly wounding public opinion or having to suffer for having done so. The procedures employed in this type of writing are multiple: obscure orientation, false citations, pseudonyms, odd expressions, inexact repetition of previously given statements. Intentional self-contradiction

21.
Leo Strauss, "Un art d'écrire oublié [A forgotten art of writing]," trans. N. Ruwet, *Poétique* 98 (1979): 244.

is the most striking quality; it functions as a kind of signal, alerting the attentive reader to try to discern the enigmatic plan of the author. The writer who makes use of this technique aims at those readers capable of thought and worthy of being trusted, while wagering that the desire for truth goes hand in hand with the desire for liberty. More precisely, this mode of writing seeks to address many kinds of readers, as if it were uniting the advantages of public communication, without risk of persecution, along with those of private communication, though the numbers involved in the latter are fewer. This kind of writing tends to create a number of communication spaces, a public one where the topic in question can be treated according to the demands of the city, and a philosophical one where the topic is treated from the viewpoint of truth. Moreover, it is not simply a matter of escaping the censure of religious or political authorities threatened by heterodox truths; it is also a matter of avoiding abuse by means of doctrinal appropriation. Preventing the degradation of a philosophical idea down to an ideological proposition can be the result of an ensemble of textual devices, maintaining a distance between the author and the fictional persona who expresses such and such a doctrine. Thus, Leo Strauss prescribes this rule for the reader: "The ideas of the author of a drama or dialogue should not, without prior proof, be identified with the ideas expressed by one or several of the characters, or with ideas shared by all the characters, or by the sympathetic characters."[22]

22. Ibid., 239.

As Michel-Pierre Edmond has justly argued, Leo Strauss's thesis is susceptible to a "weak" interpretation: this style of writing consists of a set of precautions that keep it from doing direct harm to opinion, and thus escaping eventual censure. But there is also a "strong" interpretation: opinion distrusts philosophy, and will exercise that distrust, so that philosophy will not escape opinion. "The incidents of persecution," he writes, "which are the sharp edges of opinion, against the search for truth impose not only a secret art of writing on that search, but also an art of discovering the secret."[23]

23. Michel-Pierre Edmond, "Pérsecution et politique de la philosophie," *Libre* 6 (1979): 71-72.

Now, from this point of view, the *Utopia* of Thomas More enjoys an exceptional situation: it is a text privileged by tradition, one that can put the Straussian theses to the test. In his pioneering article, Strauss himself saw Thomas More as one of the inventors of this secret art of writing, designated in the *Utopia* as the *ductus obliquus*. In fact, practically at the end of what J. H. Hexter describes as a dialogue of advice or counsel, the very principle of this technique of writing is announced, namely obliquity. But doesn't this admission abolish the text that constructs itself as oblique? Other than by responding that even the best dissimulation cannot conceal the truth, we must also remain alert to the movement of the text in which this strategy—*ductus obliquus*—will be immediately denied by those who apply it. The ruse is double. And better yet, beyond the enunciation of this oblique way within the body of the text, one can observe a veritable "*mise en scène*" of this detour, whether it be in the plurality of presences like Thomas More, who is not only the writer/author of *Utopia*—and citizen and sheriff of the illustrious city of London—but who was also once an adolescent page at the court of Cardinal Morton, and the privileged interlocutor of Raphael Hythloday in the garden of Peter Giles. Given this triple visage, how can we claim to have penetrated the author's intentions? Furthermore: the book is constructed on an obvious elaboration of the strategy that it announces. Moreover, in More's *Letter to Dorp*, roughly contemporary with *Utopia*—it was written in 1515—Thomas More pokes fun at his correspondent for seeming to find everything simple in the Scriptures. He reminds him, by way of encouraging more modesty in the man, that the Church Fathers such as Jerome and Augustine found those same Scriptures very difficult to interpret. The Fathers attributed this mode of writing to God Himself, who sought thereby to arouse the mental powers of humans. "According to them, it was God who in the height of His wisdom hid the meanings in the deepest folds of the text, in order to pique our curiosity. He hid these treasures to encourage us to dig and find them: otherwise, our lazy natures, seeing them exposed to daylight like flowers in the soil, would lose all fear of their escaping, and would mire themselves in torpor."[24] The connection seems legitimate. Following the

24.
G. Marc'Hadour, editor and translator, *Saint Thomas More* (Namur: Le Soleil levant, 1962), 85.

example of the material universe, *Utopia* would be an enigma that the author invites us to resolve.

One might risk a fundamental hypothesis regarding reading, and propose an itinerary to be followed strictly under pain of confusion, if the reader does not want to get lost in the labyrinth that has been artistically offered to us. Contrary to the majority of readers and interpreters who rush directly into Book II as if it contained the "substantive heart" of the work, instead we should pay attention to Book I which, far from being a kind of *hors-d'oeuvre* or *aperitif*, is in fact a genuine initiatory stage. Pausing before we cross over this strait from which there is no return, stopping here, staying here, dawdling here, and above all loosening up our wits here so as to be able to seize hold of the thread or threads that will allow us to follow Raphael Hythloday in the narrative of his voyage, or perhaps so as to learn how to accommodate ourselves to an unstable ground beneath our feet, one sown with traps, with vertiginous pitfalls. One cannot really read *Utopia* unless one examines the extraordinary articulation there is between Book I and Book II. Access to Book II—the utopia itself, strictly speaking, relative to the better form of government, the part of the text from which the interpreters draw their propositions to support their respective ideologies—can only be gained after a scrupulous, detailed decryption of Book I, such that the reading results in the conversion or transformation of the reader's vision. The gain involves a loss of naiveté, an increase in suspicion, and a distrust of ideological conclusions.

At this point in our journey we may appreciate the value of Leo Strauss's hypothesis in order to attempt a political reading that also accounts for the "allegorical," without dissolving the search for a better government in a spiritualistic and, ultimately, apologetic interpretation. A political reading, but of a new kind: this reading invites us to turn our attention away from doctrinal or ideological contents and toward seeing *Utopia* in terms of form, located somewhere between political philosophy and rhetoric. Thanks to the emphasis on the phenomenon of persecution, and beyond the fundamental question of opinion—which is at the same time the point of departure and the nutritive soil of both philosophy and the resistance to philosophy—this reading allows us to come to grips with both the problem of communication and the dignity of politics. Far from being a classic literary approach to utopia, this approach instead recovers the political significance of the literary question. "One cannot understand Plato's teaching," says Leo Strauss, "as he meant it if one does not know what the Platonic dialogue is. One cannot separate the understanding of Plato's teaching from an understanding of the form in which it is presented."[25] The lesson of Leo Strauss concerning the dialogues of Plato is equally important for *Utopia*—which is another way of posing the question of the "Platonism" of Thomas More. To begin with, it is best to give greater attention to the form than to the substance, "since the meaning of the 'substance' depends on the 'form.'"[26] Thus one notices a connection between the literary question and the political one: in its noblest form, communication establishes a living-together, a political community. "The literary question," according to Strauss, "the question of presentation is concerned with a kind of communication.... The study of the literary question is therefore an important part of the study of society.... The study of the literary question is therefore an important part of what philosophy is. The literary question properly understood is the question of the relation between society and philosophy."[27] And therein lies the importance of privileging Book I in our interpretation of *Utopia*, its *de jure* anteriority to what follows: the question of the communication of utopia becomes precisely the object of a classic political debate—the dialogue of counsel—at the end of which we have donned "lenses" that will allow us to read Book II. And thus we put a halt to the impatience of tyrannical readings.

Utopia is a jewel of the forgotten art of writing, and all the more precious for having been set in the form of a Roman satire; it renews that form while mixing it with the question of the better government, as Robert C. Elliot has shown in a remarkable study, one that follows other paths but joins Leo Strauss to the extent that it denies all the "positive" doctrinal

25.
Leo Strauss, *The City and Man* (Chicago: University of Chicago Press, 1978), 52.

26.
Ibid.

27.
Ibid.

appropriations. It also helps us appreciate the different interventions made by the character Thomas More.[28]

The signs of this art of writing are multiple, but we will point out a few of them: first, a work of fiction dissimulated under the guise of a travel narrative, *Utopia* uses a neologism for its title, and thereby chooses the path of ambiguity. *Utopia*, the place of no place, or rather *Udetopia*, the place of no time, or even *Eutopia*, the place of felicity where all is well: a plurality of meanings, of inspirations, of forms, as if by means of the play introduced by this plurality, *Utopia* succeeded in conquering its uniqueness, and the author in preserving his freedom. The inventor of a new model narrative—the recital of an imaginary voyage upon returning from which the traveler describes the institutions and modes of life of an ideal or a strange society—Thomas More works in several registers at once, burlesque, satire, political treatise, comedy, ideal legislation, all in order to cover his tracks most effectively. Nietzsche says that innovators make themselves mad or pretend to be in order to break free from the yoke of a given morality. And the note of madness: does it not sound in *Utopia* from the beginning? If the world's direction is toward unreason, having recourse to madness becomes wisdom, or "morosophy." Complex links between utopia and madness are evident in the work of Thomas the "morosopher": one contingent link, the fruit of chance, is the patronym of the author and the Greek word *moria*, which designates folly. Erasmus wrote *The Praise of Folly* at More's house, and with his advice. If we can believe the sketch Erasmus left in a letter to Ulrich von Hutten in 1519, the genius of satire was Thomas More's "demon." "Since childhood," wrote Erasmus, "he was always making plays on words, to the point where one would have thought that joking was the principal object of his existence.... Every jest, even if he was its target, delighted him, so much did he enjoy any kind of humor that had the scent of subtlety or of wit."[29] Another deliberate link appears in the name of the narrator, Raphael Hythloday, or "the speaker of nonsense." Thomas More's genius flowers in this intellectual satire, and perhaps even more fully in the existential attitude of many humanists who, in the company of a small group

28.
Robert C.
Elliott,
"The Shape
of *Utopia*,"
in *Utopia*, ed.
Robert M.
Adams, Norton Critical
Edition (NY:
Norton,
1975),
177-192.

29.
"Letter from
Erasmus," in
Adams, ed.,
Utopia, 130.

of enlightened friends, known to be trustworthy and chosen beforehand, thanks to the digressions of this "Gay Science," can communicate in cloaked language that each understands, despite the institutions and the established religion in place at the time, and the control that both try to exercise over minds.

And so it is that *Utopia* is written under the sign of the ruse. The first edition, as André Prévost notes, refers to the capital city as *mentira-ae*, and refers to a senate as *in senatu mentirano*, all based on the verb *mentiri* (to lie).[30] The presence of the lie is reinforced by the distinction that Thomas More draws in his prefatory letter to Peter Giles between *dicere mendacium*, which is an ironic rhetorical technique, and *mentiri*, which involves a moral failing. As Prévost says: "*Utopia* is an immense *mendacium*, in the fantasy of the adventure story, in the irony and humor of its paradoxical affirmations, and in the very nature of the myth, always attracting us and yet always impossible to fulfill. More's subtle art seeks to multiply "falsehoods" without ever actually lying. The reader must be alert to all the feints and all the traps the author deploys."[31] *Utopia* is like a mask covering a new kind of thought, one meant to shake orthodoxy, to undermine the beliefs and institutions of its time. The "nonsense" of Raphael, his absurdities, the utopia as a narrative device functioning like the extended ruse of political thought: all these are things to which the prudent philosopher has recourse so as to make himself understood without risking the dramatic fates of Savonarola, dead on the scaffold in 1498, or Thomas Münzer, decapitated in 1525. Raphael Hythloday, returned from the land of Utopia, is presented from the outset as a kind of mixture or hybrid: he has something about him of the angel Raphael, who cures blindness, of Plato, the philosopher-traveler, the man of *logos*, and of Ulysses, the trickster who regains his kingdom by means of cunning stratagems. *Utopia*, so often presented as one of the most vigorous expressions of political rationalism, in fact has much in common with the ruses of the trickster, with his style of cunning intelligence; it sits halfway between the search for truth and the seizing of any opportunity. Moreover, for the Utopians, who detest warfare and all the values associated with it—glory, honor, both are

30. Prévost, *L'Utopie de Thomas More*, cii-cx, and 94n2.

31. Ibid., 20n5.

animal virtues in their eyes—the ruse is the supreme value. A work of wit, the ruse is the very sign or manifestation of *humanitas*. It is by "ruse and artifice" (*arte doloque*) that the Utopians overcome their enemies. Just as they disdain games of chance, they also show a predilection for those who demonstrate an ability to use guile to outflank "the vices so as to conquer them."

In all but the scholarly editions, the text offered to the reader is almost always abridged; it is amputated, cut off from the "paratexts" that frame *Utopia* (the prefatory letter, correspondence, map, the utopian alphabet, the poems, etc.). And as the reader is prevented from circling the text with its paratexts, he or she is cut off from the set of devices that make up the whole, as if modern publishers so wanted to make *Utopia* into a kind of dogma that they eliminated its ludic and initiatory aspects. There can be no interpretation of *Utopia* that fails to take into account the totality of the text and its surrounding tissue. Can anyone imagine an edition of the *Encyclopedia* that suppressed the cross-references from one article to another, one that annulled the workings of the text beneath the text?

The Articulation of the Book "and of the Book"

Given the enigma that most interpreters find in the discordance between Book I and Book II—and some have even gone so far as suggesting that there were two authors, Erasmus for the first Book and Thomas More for the second—our hypothesis will be that in following the twists and turns of Book I, we will progressively come to find, or rather to work out, as if in dispelling an illusion, the right style of reading and the right understanding of Book II.

So as not to lose ourselves in this labyrinth, let us begin by trying to describe the route we need to take across several different regions. It was thanks to a temporary interruption of a mission in Flanders, in Bruges to be precise, that More was able to benefit from some philosophical leisure and came to meet, thanks to Erasmus's introduction, Peter Giles, a humanist and member of the Republic of Letters who was also versed in affairs of state. Giles was a master in the art of friendship, and hence the inaugural portrait of him: "He is, in fact, full of goodness and learning, greeting everyone liberally, but when it comes to his friends, with so much spirit, affection, loyalty, sincere devotion, that one will find few men to match him in the offices of friendship."[32]

32.
More, *L'Utopie*, 8.

First Sequence

FIRST SCENE: Peter Giles introduces Raphael Hythloday to Thomas More one morning after Mass in Antwerp, after having told him briefly about the adventures of this sailor-philosopher, in the wake of Amerigo Vespucci.

SECOND SCENE: This is the first sequence of conversation between Thomas More, Peter Giles, and Raphael Hythloday in More's house, or rather in the garden, on a bench covered with turf. The beginning of Raphael's narrative follows the link between nature and culture: this is not a matter of a travel narrative about a fantastic land peopled by monsters and chimeras, and it is not a primitivist depiction of the golden age. Raphael's interest, as well as that of his interlocutors, is primarily in "wise institutions of people living in civilized societies."

Conforming to the storyteller role as described by Walter Benjamin, Raphael, the prototypical navigator, transmits a message from distant lands. "What the storyteller recounts, he recounts from experience, either his own or that of someone who communicated it to him. And so in turn he fashions the experience of those who listen to his story."[33] A man of good counsel, he initiates reflection, and engenders comparison of the known with the unknown. So it is with Raphael: "Assuredly, he had picked up many absurd customs among these unknown people, but just as many others that one might take as models for correcting the faults in our cities, our countries, our kingdoms."[34] The first contradiction is to be noted: More announces for his program exactly the opposite of what he

33.
Walter Benjamin, "Le narrateur" [The storyteller] in *Écrits français*, ed. Jean-Marie Monnoyer (Paris: Gallimard, 1991), 209.

34.
More, *L'Utopie*, 13.

is going to do. He announces that he will be giving priority to the Utopians over other foreign peoples, whereas in his description he will be doing the inverse.

THIRD SCENE: The first dislocation occurs here. In the course of the conversation, a veritable dialogue of counsel begins among Peter Giles, Raphael Hythloday, and Thomas More. Should Raphael, the sailor-philosopher, give some king the benefit of his knowledge and his experience, thus repeating in a sense the voyages of Plato to Syracuse? A disagreement breaks out, with Peter Giles and Thomas More pleading for the plan—having recourse to different kinds of arguments, with Peter Giles taking a utilitarian or practical view, and More taking a more noble and philosophical approach—but Raphael fiercely disagrees.

FOURTH SCENE: A second dislocation appears, in the form of a play within a play. In support of his opposition, Raphael recalls an episode from some twenty years in the past, involving the entourage of Cardinal John Morton, then Chancellor of England, to whom the young More served as page. On that day, the court of the Chancellor of England was the scene of an extremely violent discussion among, first, Raphael who, maintaining that it was better to root out the causes of theft than simply to punish it, denounced the social ills then plaguing England, and secondly, an English lawyer and a friar, both in favor of the most brutal repression of crime.

FIFTH SCENE, FIRST SEQUENCE: We return now to the dialogue on counsel between Raphael Hythloday, Thomas More, and Peter Giles. To support his position, Raphael refers to two modes of deliberation in courts: at the court of the French king, on the subject of war, which he contrasts with the methods of the Achorians; and with an unnamed king on the subject of the treasury, which he contrasts with the ways of the Macarians. SECOND SEQUENCE: The dispute shifts. Thomas More argues against Raphael by distinguishing two conceptions of philosophy, and two possible modes of communication: the direct and the indirect. But Raphael nonetheless persists in his refusal with even more vehemence, saying that he suspects such indirect methods would lead only to partial reforms and not to the radical reforging that utopian communism proposes. THIRD SEQUENCE: The terrain of the discussion changes, along with the protagonists' positions—in effect, Thomas More and Peter Giles come to represent the position of public opinion, deaf to and unable to comprehend the truth of communism. More says, "But it seems to me impossible to imagine a satisfying life when all things are held in common."[35] To this, Raphael replies with the depiction of Utopia that will put the communist idea to the test, as well as his mode of communication. In short, the question is not so much about the better government as about the better form of persuasion for bringing about a just and sound political order.

At the heart of the debate throughout Book I is the famous Platonic idea of the philosopher king expressed in *The Republic* and, in an ulterior manner, in Plato's Letter VII: "If it should turn out that neither philosophers become kings nor those who we call kings become philosophers, and if political power and philosophy do not combine … then, my dear Glaucon, there will be no respite from the evils that beset States, nor from those besetting humankind."[36] Thomas More raises this topic, addressing the question to Raphael in the course of their debate on giving counsel, giving what amounts to an attenuated, more moderate version of the philosopher who is counsellor to a prince: "Your dear Plato believes that States have no chance of being happy without philosophers becoming kings or kings becoming philosophers: how can we approach that happy condition if the philosophers do not deign to give counsel to their kings?"[37] Here we no longer ask for the union in one person of philosopher and politician, but simply the presence of a philosopher near to the prince; the task is an easier one, for it is no longer a matter of converting the prince to philosophy, or of convincing him to live the philosophical life, but simply advising him on measures "conforming with honor and justice."

Raphael, for his part, retains the platonic notion in its aporetic and paradoxical character—enunciating it arouses a wave of laughter—retaining the improbable and even uncontrollable aspects of it, much closer to what Plato emphasized in Book IV of *The Republic*: "There is no perfection possible,

35.
Ibid., 53.

36.
Plato,
La République
(Paris:
Gallimard,
1950),
5.473c-d and
4.499b;
see also Letter
VII, 326b
and 328a.

37.
More, *L'Utopie*,
39.

neither for a State nor for a political regime … until the philosophers … by good fortune find themselves by necessity, whether they like it or not, compelled to take on the interests of the State, and the latter to obey; either that or until the sons of the current kings or princes are seized with the divine inspiration of an authentic love for authentic philosophy."[38] Without "good fortune," without "divine inspiration" transforming kings into philosophers, there is no way to open a path from philosophy to power. Thus Raphael denounces Thomas More's view as impracticable, which offers itself as a soothing solution to the Platonic aporia, for between the philosopher and the king stands the insurmountable barrier of opinion. Alluding to the fall of Plato at the court of Dionysius, Raphael concludes: "If kings are not themselves philosophers, they will never submit to the advice of philosophers, imbued as they have been since infancy with false ideas, and profoundly infected by them. Plato learned this at the court of Dionysius."[39]

It is worth noting that compared to his interlocutor—in this case Thomas More—Raphael retains a dual lesson from Plato: the salvation of humankind is subordinated to the question of the union of philosophy and politics in one man, and to that of communism: "That wise man saw very clearly in advance that only one, unique path would lead to public welfare, and that was via the equal allocation of resources."[40] It is as if the difficulty had been displaced, from the communication of philosophy to the novelty of communism.

But instead of following up on the arguments of each party, let us try to see how their two positions are grounded in two strongly differentiated spaces, the space of the garden and the space of the court, and how the space of the literary—the writing of utopia, or the utopian approach—offers itself as an opening toward a possible passage, at least an attempt at one, from the truths spoken in the garden to the opinion that reigns at the court.

Book I is, in effect, constructed on this recurrent contrast between the space of the garden, the space of conversation *intra muros*, safe from observation and indiscreet listeners, and the space of the court, whether it be the recollection of the

38.
Plato,
La République,
4.499b.

39.
More, *L'Utopie*,
39.

40.
Ibid.,
52.

scene with Cardinal Morton or the ideas evoked by Raphael. Now, these two spaces designate two modes of sociality, one of which permits communication and the establishment of a living-together, while the other bars that possibility. As we have said, Peter Giles is adept at the art of friendship. The space of the garden is placed under the sign of friendship, a luminous space in which the love of virtue, reciprocal esteem, and dialogue can freely flourish. Moreover, the garden encloses that protected space in which the original links between one person and another can emerge via the exchange of the gaze, "so that each can see himself reflected in, and can recognize himself in, the other," and via the exchange of words, thanks to "that great gift of the voice and of speech, so that we may bond and fraternize better, and create through the mutual declaration of our thoughts a communion of our wills."[41]

In this space where we are "all one" rather than "all united," which is sustained not through some attraction but through the sharing of the same liberal culture, through the shared experience of beautiful things, philosophy can be communicated via its radical and paradoxical questioning, with no exposure to sanction, save the light sanction of laughter, even when it collides with a contrary opinion, like the objections of Raphael's auditors with regard to communism. Thomas More, his interlocutor, recognizes that within this excentric space, philosophical discussion can play with the most heterodox ideas without ever losing sight of concern for the common world: "These theoretical considerations are very pleasant in a familiar conversation between a few friends."[42]

Thomas More admits that things proceed very differently at the court: "How can such new speech find a way to men's hearts when they are already, in their deepest convictions, predisposed against it? … While these theoretical considerations are very pleasant in a familiar conversation between a few friends, they would have no place in the counsels of princes, where important affairs are treated with sovereign authority."[43]

The space of the court is an enclosed field upon which the relationships of domination and servitude prevail, a place where the strong confront the weak. Constructed upon an

41.
Étienne de La Boétie, *Discours de la servitude volontaire* (Paris: Payot, 1976), 119.

42.
More, *L'Utopie*, 48.

43.
Ibid., 47-48.

economics of domination, this space is also under the empire of opinion and its three constituents: pride, stupidity, and stubbornness. Raphael grounds his refusal to give counsel to the prince on the inadequacy of his speech, the speech of peace, in a universe dominated by war, and on the extraordinary resistance that opinion marshals against any new idea, whether it comes from reading or from traveling. An unwise foundation on tradition, the self-regard of the group, and the orientation toward power: such are the streams that feed the despotism of opinion. "Among the members of royal councils, everyone is so wise as to feel no need for advice from any outsider, or at least they are convinced of their wisdom enough to remain deaf to others. The opinions that win their assent are the stupidest, provided that they come from those closest to the prince, and they want to render themselves favorable in his eyes by their assent. Each believes his own ideas are the best, which is a matter dictated by nature. The crow believes its young are charming, and the sight of the baby ape is enchanting to its parents."[44]

44.
Ibid., 16.

Opinion, through its close connection to arrogance—that hellish serpent that twines itself around men's hearts in order to turn them away from the true path—opinion thus operates like the remora, that suckerfish that the ancients believed could slow down a ship by attaching itself to the keel: it prevents philosophy from taking flight and from making its voice heard.

It would seem that Thomas More and Raphael are in accord with regard to distinguishing these two spaces, in order to establish the resistance of opinion, and to conclude from that the absurdity of philosophy intervening among the princes and the powerful. But this accord is only provisional because a difference quickly arises. And here we see an essential rupture in the conversation which is, in effect, the introduction to Book II; the identity of Raphael, already opaque, becomes even more enigmatic.

Indeed, Thomas More, as interlocutor to Raphael, reaffirms that it is the duty of the latter as philosopher to make his voice heard in royal councils and to work toward the public welfare. The dialogue on counsel returns as Thomas More, like a character in Machiavelli's *Mandragola*, makes a distinction between ministerial knowledge and the scientific knowledge of "things in the real world," and thus marks a differentiation between two conceptions of philosophy, and thus between two types of philosophical intervention in the political sphere. This differentiation intersects with the one formulated in Italian humanism between on the one hand a scholastic philosophy, conceived as a philosophy *a priori*, as logic, and on the other a philosophy concerned with social matters, with the *res publica*, and conceived then as rhetoric, in the conviction that rhetoric is the necessary anchorage of philosophy in the historicity of humankind, and the conviction of the importance of language, of communication—in short, in the conviction of the importance of the relation with the other.[45] Thus this new distinction Thomas More makes, and the shift it invites, recalls the debate he had just been having in the *Letter to Dorp*, alongside Erasmus, in the name of the "grammarians and poets" against the logicians, as if Thomas More, jurist and lawyer, faithful here to Cicero, wanted to return to the topic of the separation of philosophy and eloquence.

In that letter, he sings the praises of the grammarian, that is, the man of letters, to his correspondent, who expresses only disdain for this kind of scholar. The *grammaticus*, the man of letters, has studied all the sciences without exception, and has been initiated into all the branches of knowledge, while the logician has only mastered logic. In this letter, which, according to its translator, is a "treatise on true versus false dialectic," Thomas More, in attributing to his friend Erasmus the double characteristics of rhetorician and dialectician, insists on the impossibility of separating the two disciplines. Dialectic, as he views it, would be a rhetoric of conversation; thus he adopts the Ciceronian position that rhetoric and dialectic are twin arts, and he calls upon the philosophical tradition to support the position. "Some philosophers, and not the least among them, have thought quite rightly that the difference between dialectic and rhetoric is the same as that between the wrist and the palm of the hand: what dialectic brings together into a tight bundle, rhetoric spreads out and deploys; the former is the tip of a blade that digs into the opponent, while the

45. Ernest Grassi, *Humanisme et marxisme*, trans. Jean-Claude Berger (Geneva: L'Age d'homme, 1978), 64-93.

latter is a massive and diffuse power that throws him down to the ground and overwhelms him."[46] In fact the adversary against whom Thomas More directs his sharpest arrows is the logician who, in the name of contemporary logic, different from that of Aristotle, invents a whole panoply of derisory "questions," so much nonsense, of the kind to arrest the development of young intellects and trap them into living their whole lives and wasting away within the narrow, confined universe of scholasticism. The reign of these "questionists" is all the more troubling to Thomas More in their taking over a certain theology and bringing to it a gravity that it does not merit. The deplorable effect of these logico-theological authorities is the way they cut away at the intellect's knowledge of reality, locking it up inside a universe of tortured and inconsistent chimeras "that have no relation to reality." Hence the infirmity of the apprentice logician: "Whenever he ventures outside the limits of his little courtyard, and he encounters the face of reality, so unknown to him, he stumbles back into the shadows, seized by vertigo."[47] It is not logic itself that Thomas More challenges, but a certain species of logic that turns its back on the real. "Logic itself," he sees, "as strong, as subtle as it may be, is of no use to someone whose eyes are shut to reality. When logic knows the nature of things and can extract diverse modes of expression from it, it can borrow from reality a rich array of arguments; but when it does not have a firm grasp on real things, it is paralyzed, hopelessly impotent."[48] This return to the *Letter to Dorp* is most important, for it allows us to understand that Raphael's refusal only applies when it concerns a certain definition of philosophy, that which predominates under scholasticism, under the heading of logic, itself the prey of "questionism," or as Thomas More puts it, "this school philosophy that imagines its solutions are applicable to everything,"[49] characterized by its abstract universalism and its remoteness from life. But Raphael's objection loses its force if we turn to a different practice of philosophy, or rather toward a conception of philosophy that accords importance to practice. Interlocutor Thomas More explains: "But there is another philosophy, one that is acquainted with life, one that knows its

46.
Marc'Hadour,
*Saint Thomas
More*, 57.

47.
Ibid., 94.

48.
Ibid.

49.
More,
L'Utopie,
48.

range and, when it comes to the play at hand, knows its role and performs it properly. That is the one you should use."[50] We understand this to be a philosophy that, thanks to its historical and concrete anchorage in man, assumes the theatricality of the social, of being in society, and can accept the importance of appearance in the collective lives of men. Thomas More is the Christian humanist animated by a project for radical reform, and at the same time he reaffirms the task of philosophy, the indelible concern for public things, and he also provides the *novum instrumentum* which allows a new relationship to *doxa*, that is, the *ductus obliquus*.

50.
Ibid., 49.

It is not a matter of ignoring opinion, of denying the existence of that element whose inertial power drags down new ideas and heterodoxies. Nor is it a matter of imposing, as an arrogant philosophy would, "a strange and roundabout discourse upon an audience who you know in advance will not change their beliefs."[51]

51.
Ibid.

But while the duplicity of opinion, and its weight, present an obstacle to the right path, it does not follow that one must capitulate to it or give up trying to outmaneuver it. One must know how to adapt to the scene the world presents, not to consent to its madness, but to hold a mirror up to it so that, out of the complex play of illusions and tricks, unexpected and unpredictable changes may begin to emerge. "While you cannot root out erroneous opinions, this is no reason to remove yourself from public affairs."[52] This new method is suggested to us at the same time as the guiding thread we will need for reading Book II. "It is better to proceed by indirect approaches toward your goal so that, if you do not come to a good solution, you have at least led people to the least bad one possible. For how can things be made perfect until people are perfect, which I do not expect to find will be the case tomorrow?"[53]

52.
Ibid.

53.
Ibid.

The paradox of utopia is that it is thanks to its exteriority—its founder, Utopus, deliberately cut his country apart from the continent—thanks to this separation which involves an absence of relationships, and thus puts opinion inside parentheses, that the author of *Utopia* can begin to establish an unexpected relationship between the luminosity of utopia, its clarity and light, and the opacity of our world. Its insularity, its apartness from the continent, the choice of a no-place—*nusquama, nowhere*—is what permits the author to erect a fragile walkway between the two. This casts a new light on the words of the poet Paul Celan concerning utopia: "A not-outside of man— but within a sphere directed toward the human, excentric," as Emmanuel Levinas cites in *Noms propres*.[54] What then is the literary space itself, the fabulation of utopia, if not the diverted path itself, *in actu*, intended to outmaneuver prejudices, to turn them aside so as to open up hearts that have become hardened, to awaken minds that have become numbed? Hence this new tack, this new approach whose nature is to allow philosophical truths in, those truths sought and spoken in the secret space of the garden—there, where men who are genuinely concerned for the world can be oriented toward the Good—to open up a space, tortuous and indirect though it may be, within the non-philosophical world or worse, the world biased against philosophy. It is a double literary space, that of the text of Book II but also that of the paratexts, emerging from the protective garden, where the wisely arranged presence of friends, here at the book's threshold, accompany and support Thomas More at the moment when he speaks aloud those dangerous words: "Go forth, my book!"

Given the mode of reading we have been detailing, *Utopia* takes on the status of being a true rhetorical invention: thanks to the dialogue on giving counsel in Book I and to the questions debated there, we can see that for the "poet" Thomas More, Book II is an attempt at a new mode of persuasion. For Thomas More, the author of *Utopia* and not now the interlocutor in the dialogue, the character of Raphael represents a kind of mask, and in his pre-utopian and utopian journeyings with multiple detours, he becomes a textual device capable of breaking through the resistances of *doxa*, those of his contemporary readers against communism, as well as our own resistances, and of helping us recover the kingdom.

But, the attentive reader may object, how can Raphael's narrative in the garden in the afternoon be the implementation of the *via obliqua* described in the morning, while Raphael at

54.
Levinas, "De
l'Être à l'Au-
tre," 63.

the end of Book I vehemently refuses to take the approach his interlocutor, Thomas More, had suggested? That refusal is made first in the name of philosophy: "Asking me to do this is asking me to remedy the madness of others by raving madly myself. For, if I want to say what is true, I cannot say what is the contrary. Is telling lies the business of the philosopher? Perhaps it is, but it certainly is not mine."[55] Then follows a refusal in the name of the teachings of Christ: "If we must dismiss as foolish and crazy all the things that human wickedness claims are outlandish, we would have to dismiss, even among Christians, most of the teachings of Christ, and he so firmly forbade us to hide them that he commanded his disciples to go preach from the rooftops what he had whispered in their ears. The essential points of his doctrine are even further removed from the ways of the world than my discourse was."[56] Finally, he refuses in the name of effectiveness: "With regard to that roundabout approach you suggest, I cannot see where it might lead. You want me to proceed in that manner and if I cannot improve things, at least treat of them in such a way as to make them no worse. But in such councils, one cannot beat around the bush, or close one's eyes."[57] Raphael is careful to distinguish among various cases: on the one hand, proposing resolutions that conform to justice in the deliberations of a royal council— which correspond precisely to the three difficulties just enumerated, each of which is sparked by Raphael's evocation of a foreign people and their wise institutions: the repression of theft with the Polylerites, the question of war and peace among the Achorians, to the southeast of the island of Utopia, and the question of the royal treasury with the Macarians, also located close to the island of Utopia. And on the other hand, the announcement of three new concepts, all equally unheard of—Plato's imaginary Republic, the practices of the Utopians, and the message of Christ. In every case, the roundabout approach will not work; in the case of a reform, no improvement can come about, because he who wants to play by this ruse risks falling, without being aware of it, into his own trap; and as for the battle against the world's "misoneism," all Raphael needs to do is recall the words of Christ and his prohibition.

55.
More, *L'Utopie*, 49.

56.
Ibid., 50.

57.
Ibid., 50-51.

The objection raised by the attentive reader would therefore appear a legitimate one; but we still must look carefully at the arguments opposing Raphael.

And first we must note a significant contradiction between the principle of Raphael's refusal as expressed at the end of Book I, and what his actual practice was when in a council. Did he not employ that very same roundabout approach once at the court of the Chancellor of England, in the presence of the adolescent Thomas More? In order to shake up the dominant opinions regarding how to eliminate theft, he gave the example of the Polylerites who, by a wise combination of institutions, managed to succeed in preventing theft rather than punishing it. In this sense, Thomas More, the theoretician of the oblique approach, is merely the disciple of Raphael, whose practice he had witnessed.

The contradiction only increases when we see that Raphael's stratagem did in fact lead to a relatively successful outcome, because the Cardinal suggested that capital punishment could be deferred, and the criminals could be put to mandatory labor. Raphael's narrative and the effects that followed upon his description of the ways of a foreign nation certainly undermine his own condemnation of the oblique approach. And from the two other cases, according to Raphael, those relating to the Achorians and the Macarians, nothing could be expected. Again, we must distinguish between two forms of reception, the one evoked by Raphael's argument, that is the refusal of advising a court, and the other which comes about in the course of the conversation. The reference to these three distant peoples, two of which are neighbors to the island of Utopia, works like a kind of utopian crescendo, like a kind of initiation preparing his listeners to hear, despite their hesitations, no longer just a narrative about reforms but the supreme new idea, the Utopian one, the abolition of private property.

So, if we accept the "falsity" of a theory of esoteric writing, as Michel-Pierre Edmond, invites us to—"a Platonic dialogue constructing the theory of the Platonic dialogue abolishes itself as dialogue at the same time"[58]—we are in a better position to discern, as we suggested earlier, the strategic

58.
Edmond,
"Persécution
et politique
de la
philosophie,"
72.

function of Raphael's entrenched opposition to the oblique path, within the economy of the textual device constructed by Thomas More, an opposition that itself gets caught up in the problems of obliquity. On Raphael's side, announcing that refusal is essential, the condition of the possibility of the reception of his narrative; and for the success of Thomas More's design, in order for the struggle with the reader's resistances to win out, it is necessary that the reader never suspect Raphael of having gone over to the oblique side, nor—therefore—that his narrative is to have any immediate application.

Doubtless, this invention of *Utopia*, paradigm of a new approach to the relationship between society and philosophy, must be seen in connection with the rehabilitation of rhetoric addressed by Thomas More a little before the completion of his work, in the *Letter to Dorp* of 1515. *Utopia* is one of the finest fruits of the tradition to which Thomas More turned during his debate with the logicians, so well analyzed in Martin Fleisher's book on the links between radical reform and political persuasion in More. "In this perspective, as well as in the preference he accords to rhetoric to the detriment of dialectic, More is closer to the tradition of Isocrates, Cicero, and Quintilian. Human communication requires the use of words appropriate to the occasion and to the object. That a well-formed discourse also gives pleasure constitutes its merit, and helps it accomplish its other functions. Since its origins, this tradition has thought of eloquence as 'substantive' as opposed to merely decorative or ornamental. Isocrates unites rhetoric and wisdom: rhetoric is enlarged to the point of entailing philosophical questions."[59] This goes hand in hand with the case of Thomas More privileging practical reason over theoretical. *Utopia* becomes an exemplary contribution to what Martin Fleisher, insisting on the Christian context, calls the dynamic of communication.

At this point in our journey, what is the status of Book II? In terms of reading *Utopia*, we can first affirm that it is not a depiction of the golden age. *Utopia* stands aside from what Immanuel Kant, in his *Conjectural Beginning of Human History* (1786), called that "vain nostalgia" that is aroused by

59. Martin Fleisher, *Radical Reform and Political Persuasion in the Life and Writings of Thomas More* (Geneva: Droz, 1973), 98.

the phantom of a golden age; that is, a state in which humans, freed from luxury, are supposed to have satisfied the basic needs of nature and lived in perfect equality and perpetual peace, a state in which "we enjoy life fully, exempt from worry, either sunk in laziness and daydreaming, or making eyes at each other like children."[60]

The happiness that the Utopians enjoy is that of a civilized society that has already faced work and war. *Utopia*, a modern vision in that sense, depicts a working community mobilized by the struggle against nature and poverty, and relying on all its members doing an equal share of the work, and so efficiently that the work day can be reduced to six hours, freeing more time for study or for cultural pursuits.

This places *Utopia* apart from the literature of escapism, but can we derive from it a program for the organization of labor? Now, we have already asserted that it is not a matter of a program, nor of a road sign providing us with directions; it is not to be taken as a model. Do we have here a failure of analysis, or rather an index of the real character of *Utopia*? And must we be content with a series of negative determinations? Our attention must be drawn to the choice Thomas More frequently makes in deploying negatives in order to urge the reader to see that there is more than one side to the question.[61] And we can thus, via this skillful ambiguity created by a variety of complex rhetorical devices, see in *Utopia* the power and the originality of a "negative utopia," not to be confused with an anti-utopia, one that adopts the negativity proper to satire, so often present in More's works, but rather one that distances itself from the positive insofar as it is "constructive," one that refuses to settle itself into solid solutions, or into theses. J. H. Hexter, thanks to lengthy, erudite research, has given us a description of the complex structure of *Utopia*, and has dated each of its constituent parts.[62] Still, one cannot reduce the late introduction of the dialogue concerning counsel, written after Book II, to a simple staging of some interior debate on Thomas More's part regarding the opportunity to become counsellor to Henry VIII. The author of *Utopia*, by what J. H. Hexter calls this "brilliant" addition, transforms his work radically;

60. Immanuel Kant, *Oeuvres philosophiques* II (Paris: Gallimard [Bibliothèque de la Pléiade], 1985), 519.

61. Elizabeth McCutcheon, "Denying the Contrary: More's Use of Litotes in the *Utopia*," in *Thomas More's Utopia* (New York: Norton, 1975), 224-230.

62. J. H. Hexter, *More's* Utopia: *The Biography of an Idea* (Princeton, NJ: Princeton University Press, 1952). See also Hexter's "The Composition of *Utopia*," in *The Works of Thomas More* 4 (New Haven, CT: Yale University Press, 1965), xv-cxxiv, especially xix-xxiii.

he creates a new perspective which succeeds in de-dogmatizing the effects produced by Raphael's narrative.

To appreciate the importance of this change, the reader should imagine for a moment what *Utopia* would have been, how one-dimensional it would have been, if it had consisted solely of the beginning of Book I, without the dialogue on counsel, and Book II, without Raphael's peroration. The oblique method is not only a means of struggling against settled opinion, which resists anything new, but also of struggling against opinion *in the making*, in the process of rigidifying, which degrades an idea or concept into ideology. The face of Arrogance is multiform; if it manifests itself among the partisans of the established order, then pride, stupidity and obstinacy will show no mercy to the partisans of the new. And even if the utopian section properly speaking, the body of Book II, functions as the presentation of the oblique path in order to remind the world, adrift at that moment in the era of the birth of capitalism, of Plato's lesson—that an equal distribution of resources is the one and only method of leading to public welfare—one nevertheless cannot reduce this vision of abolished private property to a communist scheme. The privilege the textual device enjoys has the effect of engaging the reader in a different mode of reading, one separate from a sterile ideological one. The *Utopia* of Thomas More, like most utopian productions, can only be read *cum grano salis*, in a mode where the reader accepts the text in all its ambiguity, and submits to the maieutic effect of the utopian breaking through. This is to say that it is not a matter of decrypting the ruse in order to reveal behind the utopian fabulation one or several univocal solutions, of unmasking the text only in order to lock it back up in even more constraints than the interpretations themselves visit upon it. Moreover, mastering an art of writing, as powerful as it might be, does not guarantee that even the author has control over all the possible effects, which are beyond his mastery. Witness to this is given by the strange dream Thomas More had of becoming king of Utopia, which he described in a private letter to Erasmus in December, 1516. The utopian thrust here awakens his heroism and sense of elevation. "I can hardly describe the exultation I feel at present, to the point where I feel myself enlarged, as if I had turned myself into a higher idea. It is constantly before my eyes that my Utopians always reserve the first rank for me; and what's more, I already feel myself moving forward, crowned with that diadem with the wheaten insignia, attracting curious looks because of my Franciscan habit, holding before me instead of a scepter the sheaf of wheat, and surrounded by an escort of Amaurautes. And so in great pomp I walk in front of ambassadors and princes from other nations, whose foolish pride awakens our pity, I feel, at their having come here decked out like children, weighted down in effeminate outfits, enchained with that detestable gold of theirs, laughable in their purple, their precious stones and other worthless trinkets."[63] What is more, Thomas More the jurist—his dream having ended, he returns to the tribunal—cannot ignore the legal adage, "*fraus omnia corrumpit*" [fraud negates everything]. The utopian ambiguity and *mendacium* can be associated with fraud: they make uncertainty out of everything they touch and especially, as it happens, Raphael's message. If it is true that *Utopia*, to the extent that it reflects upon the State—and it does participate in the "great statist revolution" of the sixteenth century—tends toward the juridical-political model, more democratic than authoritarian, still one cannot for all that see in it a constitutional project, or any dogmatic plan for the society of the future. Rather, it is as if Thomas More, as the title of the book might indicate, did not so much want to present his readers with "the best form of government" as to invite them to look into the topic themselves—and hence the importance of dialogue—that is, to invite them to explore the question of what humanity would be like situated within wisely ordered cities, and the question of what a just and good political order would look like. In a sense, it is a matter of making his readers less into adepts at communism and more into Utopians whose intellects have been sharpened by reading, and thus "eminently fitted to invent processes capable of improving the conditions of life."[64] This character trait attributed to the Utopians indicates, not that their society is a perfect solution, a kind of

63. Erasmus of Rotterdam and Thomas More, *Correspondance* (Sherbrooke, Québec: Center d'études de la Renaissance, Université de Sherbrooke, 1985), 46.

64. More, *L'Utopie*, 107.

model that signifies the end of history, but on the contrary that it is engaged in the endless search for a just and good political order, demonstrated in their being in a state of permanent inventing and re-inventing. Once the utopian impulse is established, the *vis utopica* liberated, the search for the better government knows no end point.

The distancing that characterizes the utopic approach operates here, so to speak, in two ways. First there is a distancing from the existing order, but there is also an equal distancing from the "positivity" whose contours are utopically drawn. What Ernst Bloch called the utopic surplus—that core irreducible to false consciousness, to the ideology of the "Above All," of the Essential—undermines the "constructive" figure, in order to give the work its full force of indeterminacy. And there we encounter another effect of the oblique approach, the play of the secret shifting so that its limits can no longer be fixed; the enigma is no longer simply that of what connection there ought to be with the text, but now instead, enigma becomes the very object of the text. The question of the good and just political order is contaminated, becoming itself enigmatic and endless.

Where does this leave the communist idea? Or rather, to remain closer to the play of the text, has Thomas More, the author of *Utopia*, succeeded in convincing the interlocutor Thomas More, via the golden glow of Raphael's mediation, of the solid foundation and the legitimacy of the equal sharing of resources, enough to have reduced the objections that interlocutor had expressed at the end of Book I? Raphael's narrative in Book II aims to overcome Thomas More's opposition to communism by approaching it obliquely: for the latter, the communal ownership of goods would lead to laziness, sedition, and killings within the State, along with the suppression of authority and social distinctions. Now, at the very end of Book II, Thomas More formulates anew a critical opposition to that principle so fundamental to the constitution of the Utopians: "Many of these things involving the customs and laws of this people," he declares, "came into my memory now and seemed even more absurd, such as their methods of waging war, their ideas of sects and religion, and especially that fundamental principle of their constitution, the communal living and sharing of resources, with no circulation of money, all of which outweighed those things that did seem brilliant...."[65] However—and this point must be heavily emphasized—he does not revert to any of the arguments from the end of Book I, as if Raphael's persuasions had removed those objections, and instead he invokes the judgement of "popular opinion," that widely admitted sentiment, which ought to surprise and alert the reader, when we recall what Thomas More in Book I had said to Raphael about the resistance of popular opinion. Communal living outweighs everything that is brilliant, magnificent, grand, majestic, everything that in "popular opinion" constitutes the glory of a State. In short, everything that had struck him as excellent is swept away by opinion. If one pays attention to the importance of satire in *Utopia*, one can observe here, as R. C. Elliott has justly noted, the use of the classical device whereby the author ironically satirizes himself and thus invalidates his own judgment.[66] These last words of Thomas More make us measure just how far he has come, in listening to Raphael, from the other Thomas More, the one who positioned himself apart from public opinion, who had a taste for everything excellent and who says now, while retaining some of the reticence he showed in the opening, "There were in this utopian republic many things that I would wish to see in our own cities. I wish for them, but I do not expect to see them."[67]

This reticence figures like the residue of the early objections, and it reveals the distance Thomas More maintains. In order to better appreciate this distance and what its object might be, without subscribing to the thesis of Eva Brann, who "reifies" this distancing and the rejection of communism,[68] we should attend to Raphael's peroration, a veritable rupture in Book II, a point at which the description of Utopian institutions gives way to prophetic speech—a change of register—and proclaims the need for an ethical order, what Emmanuel Levinas calls "nostalgia for the just." By doing so, we will discern more clearly what effect Raphael's persuasion has had on his interlocutor. Thomas More is not as much convinced

65. More, *L'Utopie*, 152.

66. Elliott, "The Shape of Utopia," 186-92. See also his *The Shape of Utopia: Studies in A Literary Genre* (Chicago: University of Chicago Press, 1970).

67. More, *L'Utopie*, 152.

68. Eva Brann, "'An Exquisite Platform': Utopia," *Interpretation* 3, no. 1 (Autumn 1972): 1-26.

about how well-founded the "communist solution" is, as he is about the excellence of two principles. If the thought of utopia, beyond this or that particular project, is essentially a thought about a difference from what currently exists, an uncontrollable, endlessly reborn movement toward a social alterity, then rather than attacking utopia on the basis of a particular program, it would be better to seek out the principles that would support it and help carry it toward that "wholly other sociality." But we must understand "principle" in the sense given by Ernst Bloch: "principle" indicates, first, the idea of a beginning, in all its power, a different beginning, and at the same time the principle is capable of leading that beginning toward the future; it is a category that shows us the direction to follow.[69] Beyond instituting a common ownership of goods, there is a more original and more urgent necessity; the principle of hope of Thomas More is, first of all, that "no one should lack more than is necessary." From the otherness of utopia, one of the most manifest signs is that "no one should have to beg or suffer poverty," or rather, "a man is sure he will not lack the necessities so long as the public granaries are full."[70] And as Adorno puts it: "The true kindness would be in the most brutal of responses: that no one will ever suffer hunger again."[71] As Hegel would later, Thomas More understood the truth of the biblical phrase, and made it his guiding star: "Seek first of all food and clothing, and the kingdom of God will open up to you."[72] What would it be to think utopia in terms of hunger, of the elimination of the hunger of "the other"? Emmanuel Levinas says, "The hunger of others awakens men from the drowsiness brought on by their own fullness and sobers them up and out of their complacency."[73]

The second principle to be investigated: utopia, over and above everything else, always leads back to the essential question: must we think of human society in Hobbesian terms, as in a constant state of war, *homo homini lupus*, man is a wolf to men? Is the sole aim of social institutions to limit the effects of that war that carries with it the destruction of the human race, or is it possible to think otherwise about the social, based on "common law," *lex communis*—or on friendship,

69.
Ernst Bloch, *Experimentum Mundi*, trans. Gérard Raulet (Paris: Payot, 1981), 171-74.

70.
More, *Utopia*, 82 and 147.

71.
T. W. Adorno, *Minima Moralia*, trans. Eliane Kaufholz (Paris: Payot, 1980), 147.

72.
Hegel, letter to Major Knebel, 30 August 1807.

73.
Emmanuel Levinas, "Sécularisation et faim," in *Archivo di filosofia* 2/3 (1976): 109.

the *societas amicorum*, as Guillaume Budé called it? Budé had read Thomas More, and his letter to Thomas Lupset of July 31, 1517 serves as a preface to the second edition of *Utopia* in 1518. The reference above to Hobbes's *Leviathan* is appropriate: More's depiction of pride has nothing to do with that desire to dominate, the endless desire for power that defines the human *conatus* according to Hobbes. Pride, the "wild beast," the "queen and mother of all evils," is the first power of resistance to friendship among men: "Prosperity in her eyes is not measured in terms of the welfare of each, but in terms of the misery of others. She would even refuse to become a goddess if she had to give up having miserable people around her to insult, to treat as slaves, whose distress serves to elevate her own felicity, people she can torture and frustrate by displaying her own riches."[74]

74.
More, *L'Utopie*, 151.

This shift from the solution or the particular program to the level of principle is essential, in that it introduces a certain plasticity, and prevents us from reading in a certain erroneous manner—that is, reading in order to detect solutions, unify them, and articulate them to the point of deducing a system which would then become a model. As we have said already, the use of the oblique approach weakens, even destroys the very idea of a solution. Because of the detours this approach deploys, and its use of various measures or devices, ideas come into view which, upon a superficial reading, appear to be presented as solutions, but instead we are encouraged to seek out the principle that animates and supports these ideas. An example is the provision according to which Utopia's great and beautiful cities "are all built on the same blueprint and look the same, to the extent that the individual sites will permit it."[75]

75.
Ibid., 58.

Of course, this privileging of sameness never fails to provoke those who hate utopia, and accuse it of insisting on uniformity, if not a kind of urban totalitarianism. But let us leave these enemies of utopia to sing their favorite old song and try instead to see behind these identical towns a vital issue, one that involves attacking pride, that queen of all evils who urges men to find their happiness in the unhappiness of others. Thus the lord or the patrician knows his own happiness only by contrasting the majesty and pomp of his dwelling with the barren huts of the local residents. It is as if distinction gave free rein to the *libido dominandi*, multiplying tenfold the pleasure of the man who wants to display his distinction. And thus the readers, instead of attacking the uniformity of towns, make their own detour and come to see, thanks to this urban politics, that they are being tempted to bring their own pride to a standstill, to examine the ground on which they stand, and to consider that the emotion of pride within themselves can in fact be reduced if its food supply is cut off. To the reader, then, falls the task of searching out behind such and such an arrangement what larger principle is in play. The result is that, far from dogmatizing the arrangement in question and setting it up as a model or solution, the reader comes to see it for what it is, a simple putting into practice of a principle, and so the reader can relativize it, asking to what extent this implementation could be varied if it did not fully satisfy its underlying principle. We must not forget that, quite the contrary to anything like a condition of stasis, the Utopians are always at work inventing a new implementation; let us not forget that, "sharpened by reading, the minds of the Utopians are eminently fitted to invent processes capable of improving the conditions of life."

The question *Utopia* poses is this: must we think of peace— and Raphael defines himself as a specialist in the "benevolent arts of peace"—as simply a suspension of or limitation on war, or instead should we see here the emergence of another principle, a more fundamental one—one separate from logic or self-preservation—the emergence of a responsibility for others? This is why Raphael turns to the subject of famine toward the end of his peroration: famine presents that moment of extreme crisis that involves self-preservation, that aggravates the conspiracy of the well-fed, or instead can lead to a sudden experience of humanity, "the transfer that moves from the memory of my own hunger to the pain others feel, and to my responsibility for the hunger of others," to use the terms of Emmanuel Levinas. The very existence of utopia: is it not the flourishing of this principle of responsibility for others? Is it not always returning us to this same question? And is this not the same question raised by one of the most inspired of modern utopianists, Pierre Leroux, who formulates the great determining question thus at the outset of his great book, *De l'humanité*: "Who are you in relation to others? Are you brothers, or are you enemies?"[76] It is only in a refutation of Hobbes, in the enunciation of an Anti-Hobbes that utopia can come into existence.

76.
Pierre
Leroux,
De l'humanité I
(Paris:
Perrotin,
1845), 5.

For one who accepts the articulation we have traced between Book II and Book I, *Utopia* will look like a rhetorical invention, a renewal of and an orchestration of the art of persuasion. But this rhetorical invention: is it not also an unsung political invention, an unprecedented intervention into the human? Instead of opposing Thomas More to Machiavelli, as a centuries-old tradition has done, we might note that the latter, in the famous Chapter XV of *The Prince* (1513), dismisses imaginary republics, while the former reactivates the Platonic tradition for the modern world—the tradition of investigating what is the best government—would it not behoove us instead to bring the two together, and to contrast them with a third figure, that of Savonarola? Is it not a matter of a critical reflection on the disarmed prophet that, in the one case, supports a critique of prophets and of their disarming, and, in the other, invents a different path, one separate from prophecy, one that is precisely the path of *Utopia*? Raphael's final peroration, with its inspired accents, is there to mark the difference between prophetic declaration and the oblique path of utopia.

The *Utopia* of Thomas More distances itself from Christian millenarianism, from chiliastic consciousness and its denial of temporality. But at the same time, does it not suggest a desire to inscribe the truth of that tradition, the *lex communis*, the search for *humanitas*, the dimension of justice, within a new political space that—thanks to the *ductus obliquus*—recognizes the other's right to existence (and the use of persuasion implies such a recognition), and the constraints upon its effectuation within time, and the patience that requires a steadfast will?

Walter Benjamin,
the Sentry of Dreams

To grant the possibility of utopia is to give in to the mad, un-conditional vow to be done once and for all with the present injustice; it is to give in to the inextinguishable thirst for justice and the *immediate*, present demand for it.

—FRANÇOISE PROUST

Utopia or catastrophe? Let us begin by noting that such is the alternative that Walter Benjamin patiently elaborates, and not the facile association of these two terms that entails so much of our contemporary resignation as well as a hatred of utopia. These are two slopes down which it is all too easy to slip.

Benjamin, who thinks in original ways, is a superb teacher on the subject of utopia, on its traditions, and indeed it is precisely because of his awareness of the rupture in tradition that he is constantly inventing new connections with the Past. He remains an incomparable guide to the *terra incognita* of those utopias that remain veiled or hidden from us by the condemnations that have showered down upon them from various sides. How else can I express the liberation I felt upon reading *Paris, capitale du dix-neuvième siècle* [*The Arcades Project*] while I was working on a study of William Morris and the "new utopian spirit"? In reading *The Arcades Project*, with its opening up of a new realm of thought, I seemed to be granted a new freedom with respect to the Marxist rejection of utopia, while neither minimizing the complexity of the Marxist critique nor failing to recognize its legitimate points, for example with regard to Saint-Simonianism. Only in the nineteenth century could such a feeling for liberty arise, such a new openness to utopia, as in "The Samarez Strike" (1863-65), a philosophical poem by Pierre Leroux. Here utopia is described as a truly dynamic experience, close to ecstasy, and Leroux has a solid grasp on the relation between a new blossoming of the utopian and the "essence of the nineteenth century." And even better: he explores the relation between the idea of utopia and the idea of the human, as if utopia both enacted and clarified the enigma of human relationships.

Walter Benjamin belongs to those "happy few" who took up that same exploration in the twentieth century.[1]

1.
Let us trace the main stages in the voyage to Utopia found in *Paris, capitale du dix-neuvième siècle: Le livre des passages*, in the "arcades" sequence [the "Convolutes" section]: G: Expositions, publicity, Grandville. K: Dream cities and dream houses, dreams of the future, Jung and anthropological nihilism. U: Saint-Simon, railroads. W: Fourier. X: Marx. k: the Commune. p: anthropological materialism, the history of sects. All are in Walter Benjamin, *Paris, capitale du XIXe siècle* (Paris: Cerf, 1989).

The very phenomenon of the arcades, with their polymorphous character mixing Old and New—their imitation of the ancient architectural styles along with their innovative alliance of steel and glass—is this not in itself a doorway into utopia? In a preparatory note from 1935, Benjamin referred to "these arcades as dream image and as collective desire."[2] Benjamin's real power resides in his creation of a possible encounter with utopia as something to be taken seriously at last, seen as a form of "savage thought" within modernity, but being neither fetishized, nor domesticated, nor depreciated. Through his unique research for the interminable writing of the "arcades book," Benjamin gave himself the task of gathering up, maintaining and preserving a fragile promise—without becoming entangled in disenchantment—a promise not so much of happiness as of redemption, in the sense Adorno meant at the end of *Minima Moralia*: "The only philosophy which can be responsibly practiced in the face of despair is the attempt to contemplate all things as they would present themselves from the standpoint of redemption. Knowledge has no light but that shed on the world by redemption."[3]

"The sentry of dreams." The phrase comes from Victor Hugo's *L'Homme qui rit*, and refers to the role played by Ursus, the wandering cynic *saltimbanque* philosopher, with regard to his pupil Gwynplaine, whose fantasies of social justice Ursus considers dangerous in a society based on the domination of lords. "A philosopher is a spy, and Ursus, sentry of dreams, kept a close eye on his pupil."[4] Walter Benjamin is a sentry of dreams, a philosopher-spy in another sense. As he teaches us to turn our attention to the collective dreams of the nineteenth century, he works at the same time to keep us from the unhealthy fascination that those dreams are still capable of exercising upon us. "We must awaken ourselves from what had been the existence of our parents."[5]

If Benjamin succeeds in offering us another vision of the nineteenth century, one removed from a narrow rationalism, an eclecticism or a positivism, if he presents the century to us in all its luxuriousness and all its extravagance without any censure, at the same time he also teaches us to identify the

2.
Ibid., 891.

3.
T.W. Adorno,
Minima Moralia,
230.

4.
Victor Hugo,
L'Homme qui rit
(Paris:
Gallimard,
1978), 295.

5.
Benjamin,
Paris, 893.

multiple phantasms that haunt him, so we will be better able to resist them. Here we see the central difference between Benjamin and Louis Aragon in his *Paysan de Paris* (1926), though that was a book that thrilled the susceptible heart of Walter Benjamin. In his "First Notes" (June 1927-December 1929), Benjamin situated his work in the following manner: "Distinguish this work and its direction from those of Aragon: while Aragon always stays in the domain of the dream, here it is important to locate the constellation of awakening. While an impressionistic element—'mythology'—persists in Aragon … here it is a matter of dissolving mythology in the space of history. This can only be done … by awakening a knowledge not already conscious of the Past."[6]

We can call him the sentry of dreams, then, because, being something of a cynic philosopher, it is important for Benjamin to reveal the "counterfeit money" of the nineteenth century's dreams, and in doing so he describes himself as the philosopher with an axe. In his "First Notes," he describes his project in this way: "Clear the ground in those areas where heretofore only madness has grown in abundance. Go forward with the sharpened axe of reason, looking neither to the right nor to the left, so as not to succumb to the horror deep in the virgin forest that attempts to seduce us. Every plot of ground one day needs to be cleared by reason, to have its undergrowth of delirium and myth weeded out. This is what needs to be done for the uncultivated fields of the nineteenth century."[7]

The reader of Benjamin cannot help but notice over and over again—though it comes out in different ways according to the requirements of the moment—an irreducible tension between the quasi-deadly fascination exerted by the dreams of modern mythology, and the will to break out of the dream, to pull oneself away from the nocturne of the nineteenth century in interpreting the dream—that is, in constructing a dialectical image. The title for the first text from 1928-29 was "Faery Dialectic." Even though this title, revealing that tension, was later abandoned, it is worthwhile to remember it so as not to lose sight of the considerable ambiguity of the arcades and of the significations attached to them. "The arcades twinkle

6.
Benjamin, *Paris*, 842. See also 893: "Opposition to Aragon: connect all this to the dialectic of awakening instead of remaining asleep in 'dream' or in 'mythology.'"

7.
Ibid., 839.

in the Paris of the Empire like faery grottoes." "A whisper of glances fills the arcades, where knowing winks are exchanged with nothingness."[8] But far from cultivating that ambiguity or fixing it, Benjamin must construct "the dialectical structure of awakening." Unlike Pierre Leroux, who with his singular narratives tries to tease out the essence of the nineteenth century, with a critical intention, Benjamin, in another historical situation, facing practical demands and under the sign of urgency, treats the nineteenth century "like a dream from which one must awaken: a nightmare that weighs upon the present, even as its charm remains unbroken."[9]

And so it is within this space, between fascination and awakening, that Walter Benjamin is posted as sentry of dreams. An incomparable guide, he helps us penetrate into the unexplored forest of utopias, not in order to give in to their magic, but to hunt down and chase out the mythology or delirium that haunts and destroys them. And not so much to assure the victory of the established, inherited view of reason as to preserve the liberating spark that animates them and, at the same time, to help give birth to a new, "enlarged" concept of reason, one sufficiently adventurous to accept some intersection with a kind of savage thought that both marks the limits of reason and points out its blind spots. As he puts it directly in an essential fragment from the "arcades book," the criticism he invites us to practice, far from being simply destructive, instead defines itself as cathartic, even salvational; it partakes of a double movement, seizing upon the marks of unreason inscribed within reason, but also grasping hold of the traces of reason present in unreason.[10]

The most overt recognition of the central character of utopia comes in this passage: "It is not just the fact that the forms that the collective dream of the nineteenth century took must no longer be neglected, and not just the fact that they characterize this collective in a much more decisive fashion than anything else, but that if they are carefully interpreted, they have the highest practical importance; they provide us with a glimpse of the sea we are trying to navigate, and the shore from which we push off. It is precisely here that the

8.
Ibid., 870, 874.

9.
R. Tiedemann, introduction to Benjamin, *Paris*, 17.

10.
T. W. Adorno, *Trois études sur Hegel* (Paris: Payot, 1979), 84.

'critique' of the nineteenth century, to put it in a single word, must intervene."[11]

The sea upon which we navigate? The image ought to make us take notice. To use a metaphor Hannah Arendt used in her essay on Walter Benjamin, perhaps this sentry of dreams is also a fisher of pearls, one who dives into the ocean's greatest depths in order to wrest something rare and precious and bring it up to the surface.

In listing the texts relevant to utopia,[12] I would add extracts from the correspondence between Adorno and Benjamin, and especially the letters from the summer of 1935, which constitute a veritable philosophical debate on the question of utopia and the interpretation that Benjamin proposes in his Exposé of 1935. In fact, the question of utopia for Benjamin, the place he accords it, the vigilance he exercises over it—these only achieve their full dimensions in the light of that debate with Adorno.

What were the effects? Reading these texts, are we justified in concluding that utopia has disappeared by the time of the Exposé of 1939? Or should we consider, instead, that Benjamin was stimulated by Adorno's critique and also by reading Blanqui's *L'Éternité par les astres*, written in 1872, and that Benjamin elaborated a different way of thinking about utopia in the course of these years—a new utopian spirit—such that the opposition of utopia or catastrophe was transformed into a "Diane" that "rattles the kitsch of the previous century," and the result is an evocation of utopia *against* catastrophe?

THE EXPOSÉ OF 1935

Utopia plays an essential role in the Exposé of 1935. In a sense, the opening text, "Fourier or the Arcades," can be read as a critical commentary on the Michelet phrase used as an epigraph: "Every epoch dreams of the next one. The future! The future!"

Benjamin's method consists of establishing a correlation between an aspect of Parisian reality, in this case the novel architecture of the arcades, and "a man who in a sense has dreamed

11.
Benjamin, *Paris*, 408.

12.
This corpus includes, apart from the texts cited above and extracts from *The Arcades Project* concerning utopia, the reports on the project given at different moments in the process of its elaboration, such as: 1) the faery dialectic, the Exposé of 1928-29 with the first notes attached to it; 2) the Exposé of 1935; 3) the Exposé of 1939. To these texts we could add the evidence provided in *Baudelaire*, and Benjamin's last text, "Sur le concept d'histoire," as well as his "L'oeuvre d'art à l'époque de sa reproducibilité mécanisée."

13.
Dolf Oehler,
"Paris, capitale
du XIXeme
siècle: la con-
struction de
l'histoire chez
Benjamin," in
Paris au XIXe
siècle: Aspects
d'un mythe
littéraire (Lyon:
Presses Uni-
versitaire de
Lyon, 1984),
15.

14.
"Marx details
the causal
correlation
between
economy and
culture. Here,
the important
thing is the
expressive
correlation.
The import-
ant thing is
not the eco-
nomic genesis
of culture, but
the expression
of the eco-
nomic within
the culture."
Benjamin,
Paris, 476.

15.
Cited in
Tiedemann,
introduction
to Paris, 15.

16.
Benjamin,
Paris, 410.

17.
Ibid., 35.

18.
Ibid., 68.

these phenomena, or at least, whose work or whose biography would allow the phantasmagoric quality of those phenomena to come back into existence."[13] The correlation suggests how much Benjamin privileged an expressive schema, to the detriment of a purely causal one, for in his view, every expression that entails elaboration cannot be reducible to the simple effect of causality. And hence the distant stance he adopted with regard to his theory of reflection.[14] Expression, elaboration: in short, a complex task that requires the interpreter to turn his attention to the dimension of the imaginary, and more, toward the dimension of the dream, so that a veritable oneiric model comes to intervene in his own analysis. "To understand the arcades in their depths, we bury them in the deepest oneiric strata."[15] To give a complete account of an epoch includes giving an account of its dreams, "of the oneiric consciousness of the collective." Benjamin writes, "The collective expresses above all the conditions of its life. These latter find their expression in dream and their interpretation in awakening."[16] Thus understood, the architectural creation of the arcades reveals itself as fundamentally ambiguous, in the image of the nineteenth century, of which they are a kind of condensation.

On the one hand, this new form of life falls under the jurisdiction of Marxist analysis: its appearance corresponds to the conjunction of two conditions, commerce in building materials and the beginnings of the use of steel in construction. The arcades belong, unquestionably, to the reign of commodity merchandise. "The arcades are the destined centers of commerce in luxury merchandise."[17] Or, again: "The arcades, temples of merchant capital."[18] On the other hand, the arcades, in their ambiguity reflecting the century's own ambiguity, function like phantasmagoria, that is, the ensemble of the methods that make phantoms visible and capable of being spoken about in public, thanks to optical illusions.

"In the immediacy of the perceptible presence," the phantasmagoria, in its character of illusion, effects a transfiguration that turns the human gaze away from reality. The phantasmagoria casts a spell over the spectator, a fascination, such that the capitalism whose expression it is appears enchanting and the merchandise an enchantress. Space where the spectral appears—the wax museums chose to locate there—the arcades, that world of mirrors and "stifling enchantment," exercise a maleficent charm over anyone who surrenders to them. The ambiguity of the arcades is first of all in the space reinforced by wealth and the endless play of mirrors. That world of mirrors, at the same time as it arouses desire—the gaze of things—"a whisper of glances fills the arcades,"[19] and "in its uninterrupted metamorphosis"[20] gestures toward nothingness. The winks there have a double meaning. "There is nothing here that, at the moment when one least expects it, fails to open an eye and quickly close it in a rapid wink."[21] Thus the strolling about one does in an arcade takes place as if on a ghostly pathway. Within this specular universe, the phantasmagoria, the source of the magic, of paralyzing charm, puts into play, by virtue of the illusion it creates, the process of idealizing the merchandise. With the revolution will come the power to break this evil spell and give life to what is hidden within death and nothingness. Benjamin believes that "only the revolution will introduce free air into the city definitively. The fresh air of revolutions. The revolution will free the city from the spell."[22]

The ambiguity of the arcades redoubles, for one cannot limit their connection only to the imaginary, only to the phantasmagoria. Linked to the deepest oneiric stratum, the arcades, paradigm of modernity, allow us a glimpse of a "disturbing strangeness" in which dreams and phantasmagoria are mingled. The nineteenth century is no exception to the law of generations: "Each epoch has one side turned toward dreams, which is its childhood side. The residue of the preceding century is readily apparent in the arcades."[23] The vertiginous muddle that results, within the oneiric consciousness of the collective, acts like a permanent process of exchange between phantasmagoria and utopia: if the phantasmagoria reveal a utopian tonality, is it not due to the enchantment of the world of merchandise within the play of all those mirrors acting upon the different dream of happiness of each generation? And inversely, is it not true that utopia itself, the historical figure of the dream, is affected by the styles of the phantasmagoria?

19.
Ibid., 557.

20.
Ibid., 874.

21.
Ibid.

22.
Ibid., 440.

23.
Ibid., 405.

FOURIER, OR THE ARCADES

Walter Benjamin's strength, as well as his genius, resides in having invented a new constellation in which the magic of the arcades as well as the luxuriance of utopia have mingled into a "promise of happiness." While traditional interpretation associates the arcades with the flâneur, Benjamin's poetic thinking separates them from the flâneur's strolling and instead links them with the street gallery of the phalanstery.[24] The arcades, through their association with dream, point irresistibly toward utopia. And the inverse is true as well: utopia does not escape the empire of nineteenth century phantasmagoria. Because of this ambiguity, this muddle, utopia becomes the place/no-place in which sleep and myth, dream and awakening endlessly struggle. Benjamin declares, "Capitalism was a natural phenomenon in which a new sleep descended upon Europe, accompanied by a reactivation of mythic powers."[25] Given this analysis, which is inseparable from a fight against myth, the figure of dependence and heteronomy, we can appreciate the entirely new importance Benjamin grants to "the forms that reveal the collective dream of the nineteenth century," and we can better appreciate the originality of his approach. But unlike the surrealists, he is on guard against the seduction of the myths and their inexorable drift toward nothingness, and he is just as careful neither to reject nor neglect the forms of the dream, those oneiric visions of the collective through which the drift toward death can be overcome.

"The dream secretly awaits the awakening, and he who dreams only gives himself over to death in a provisional manner, waiting for the moment when he can detach himself from it by ruse and by strength. It is the same for the dreaming collective, whose children provide a happy occasion for awakening."[26] Taking these dream forms seriously, he set himself to welcoming them, not in their immediacy, but by lifting up the masks they wore, under which lay hidden "a signal of their true historical existence." The author announces that "decoding that signal is what my work will attempt."[27] We see how fruitful the new correlation Benjamin forges between Fourier and the arcades

24.
B. Lindner, "Le *Passagen-werk*," in *Walter Benjamin et Paris*, ed. H. Wismann (Paris: Cerf, 1986), 19.

25.
Benjamin, *Paris*, 408.

26.
Ibid., 407.

27.
Ibid., 408

will be, and its impact on his whole project. Indeed, if we note the constant identification of the arcades with the nineteenth century, we see that interpreting the preceding century must have occupied his attention entirely, making him intensely sensitive to the utopian vein that is present throughout the century. And this is not to accept it as it manifests itself, nor simply to register it, but to construct from it a constellation saturated with tensions, from which the dialectical image must eventually emerge.

Unlike Ursus, the sentry of dreams is not there to oversee the perhaps dangerous dream of justice with regard to the existing order, but he remains there to keep watch for the encounter, in the dreams of the collective, with mythic forces that labor to prolong the slumber of the capitalist universe—and to keep watch for that fragile gleam that can suddenly lead to awakening, and pull away from the enchantment of the nineteenth century.

Such is the difficult, demanding position from which Walter Benjamin approaches utopia, proposing his critical-salvational interpretation. Within utopia, considered as a form of the collective dream, he distinguishes two strata.[28]

First, the historical stratum: the appearance of a new mode of production corresponds, in the collective consciousness, to a new epoch of images of desire (*Wunschbilder*). Let us note that a new mode of production, through the desires it engenders, gives rise to representations of a better society. The simple representation thus becomes an image of desire (*Wunschbild*) that carries a signature: "This is how it should be."[29] Through these images, the collective seeks as a whole to suppress and transfigure the failures of the social product as well as the deficiencies in the social order of production.[30] This is the first ambiguity of these forms, since they include within themselves a critical import—an aspiration toward a better order—and a mythological dimension, as it manifests itself in the process of transfiguration. Mixed images of surplus, for the Old mixes with the New, and it is by virtue of that mixing that utopias participate to some extent in the phantasmagorias of the nineteenth century. We must also note that for Walter Benjamin, the utopia involved with images of desire as such does not

28.
Here, we are concerned with the part of the Exposé of 1935 explicitly devoted to utopia. The preparatory notes for the Exposé contain two other versions of this passage; we will make reference to them later.

29.
Or, "Desires create nothing, but they do form an image of that which ought to be created, and they conserve it faithfully." Bloch, *Le Principe espérance* I, 64. Without getting into the question of what connections there may be between Bloch and Benjamin, it does seem legitimate to refer to the pages that Bloch has devoted to the image of desire.

30.
Benjamin, *Paris*, 36.

simply designate a particular text or certain practices, but more importantly a general tone that leaves its trace in "a thousand configurations of life, from durable edifices to the passing fashions."[31]

31. Ibid.

A second, ahistorical stratum comprises what is in a sense the invariable kernel of utopia, as if every utopian formulation had a secret link to the golden age. In order not to oversimplify the interpenetration of the Old and the New, we must see that in Benjamin's text, the Old means not only the most recent past—the old mode of production—but also a past that is old in another sense, a sense that goes beyond history. These images, from an extremely distant past, allow the collective to succeed in separating itself from the recent past, a distancing function that was known to that prehistoric past. It is by this complex path that images of desire arouse, or perhaps reactivate, the image of a classless society. "These tendencies turn the imagination (impelled by the New) back toward the most ancient past. In the dream where every epoch keeps its gaze upon images of the epoch to come, the latter appears mingled with elements of prehistory (*Urgeschichte*), that is, of a society without classes. The experiences relative to such a society, stored in the collective's unconscious, by interpenetrating with the New, give birth to utopia."[32] Thus it is with Fourier's utopia. It finds its "most intimate impulsion" in the appearance of machines—the historical stratum, which manifests itself in a veritable machinery of the passions. However, and such is the state of the ahistorical stratum, Fourier's utopia reactivates the image of a classless society. "This machinery composed of men creates a land of Cockaigne, the most ancient symbol of achieved desires, to which Fourier's utopia gives new life."[33]

32. Ibid.

33. Benjamin, Exposé of 1935, in *Paris*, 37.

The Benjaminian thesis of the dualist structure of utopia both underlines its composite nature and at the same time puts the interpreter, ready to welcome it, on guard against any unequivocal judgments, whether entirely favorable or entirely unfavorable. The sentry of dreams is invited to practice a critical hermeneutic that, far from dismissing or dissolving utopia, instead engages with it by separating it from myth, and thus liberates its emancipatory potential.

This work seems even more necessary for the interpreter than it did in the first preparatory version of the Exposé of 1935. There, Walter Benjamin had insisted on the fantastic dimension of those images of desire, strongly marked by the interpenetration of the Old and the New. "This interpenetration," he writes, "takes its fantastic character above all from the fact that the Old never detaches entirely from the New in the flow of social development, and that the New, in its effort to distinguish itself from the Old, gives new life to primitive, archaic elements. The utopian images that accompany the blossoming of the New constantly recur and refer back, simultaneously, to a very distant past."[34] This recurrence: does it not seem to be a ruse of the utopian imagination? In the same text, Benjamin writes: "The New, in order to take on the form of an image, must always associate its elements with the elements of a classless society."[35] The main function of this evocation of the most distant past would be to separate itself from the recent past, rather than laying down broad outlines of a project for the future.[36] In the face of a given utopia, it is best therefore to "decode," beneath the fantastic mask with which it covers itself, the signal of a real opening. If Fourier, in his depiction of a future society, betrayed reactionary tendencies in removing the arcades from the social sphere in order to make them into simple living spaces, he nonetheless avowed "a spectacular vision of the human being" that goes well beyond any program of educating the passions.

At the origins of Walter Benjamin's thesis one can detect—as M. Löwy in *Rédemption et utopie* did[37]—a reference to Bachofen, author of *Le Matriarcat*, to which Benjamin was going to devote an essay, planned for *La Nouvelle revue française*.[38] In the course of a portrait contrasting or alternating between the sage dilettante lord, the Basel patrician, and the romantic devoting all his attention to the Matriarchy, Benjamin insisted on the presence of Bachofen in his research into sociologists, whether they were anarchists (Élisée Reclus), or socialists (Paul Lafargue, the Marx type): "Bachofen studied, in depths never before explored, the sources that through the ages have nourished the libertarian ideal that Reclus called out for.... The indisputable

34.
Benjamin, *Paris*, 904.

35.
Ibid.

36.
S. Buck-Morss, *The Dialectics of Seeing: Walter Benjamin and the Arcades Project* (Boston: MIT Press, 1991), 116.

37.
M. Löwy, *Rédemption et utopie* (Paris: P.U.F., 1988), 148 ff.

38.
"Johan Jacob Bacofen," in Walter Benjamin, *Écrits francais*, 91-113.

39.
Ibid., 107.

40.
On this point,
see the very
enlightening
article by M.
Pezzela, '"Image
mythique et im-
age dialectique':
Remarques sur
le *Passagenwerk*,"
in *Walter Ben-
jamin et Paris*,
517-528. He
writes, on 518,
"The stakes
in this debate
were decisive. It
was necessary
to elaborate a
reflection on
myth, on the
personal and
the collective
unconscious,
on the symbolic
structure of the
imaginary, all
with the power
to oppose the
culture of Nazi
irrationalism. It
was necessary to
avoid an un-nu-
anced opposi-
tion between the
imaginary forces
that Bachofen
had considered,
and every form
of rational
consciousness.
But it was also
necessary to
go beyond the
limits of a
wholly negative
spiritual attitude
with regard to
the very notion
of the symbolic
image."

41.
T. W. Adorno
to Walter
Benjamin, 2
August 1935,
in Benjamin,
Correspondance,
1929-1940 II,
170-182.

fact that certain matriarchal communities had a highly developed democratic order along with ideas of civic equality—this had attracted Bachofen's attention. Communism, to him, seemed inseparable from gynocracy."[39]

Now, beyond the thematic of the classless society, so important in the Exposé of 1935, the question of myth was posed anew for Benjamin, this time through the interpretation of Bachofen. At this point, he would have to invent a narrow path that would allow him to take into account what symbolic expression implied without ceding any ground whatsoever to the harebrained fascist ideas of some of his contemporaries, and without taking refuge in a passive reception of "originary images."[40]

Might one conclude this analysis by stating that given the thesis of the two strata, of the dualistic structure of utopia, Walter Benjamin opened up, beyond the enchantment of capitalism, a passage (or arcade) between the Eden of a classless society and the emancipated society of the future?

It was upon this relation between the "archaic" and utopia, among others—as if primitive communism were the unavowed secret of all the utopias in history—that Adorno was going to base his critique in the letter of August 2, 1935, concerning the first Exposé of Walter Benjamin.

THE CONTROVERSY WITH ADORNO

Adorno's critique in the letter of August 2, 1935 concerns essentially four points.[41]

I. The author of *Negative Dialectics* begins by rejecting the epigraph that Benjamin had chosen to introduce his interpretation of utopia. This was the phrase from Michelet: "Every epoch dreams of the following one. The future! The future!" The phrase was no doubt seductive to Benjamin because, to its simple insistence on the future, the dominant theme of the nineteenth century that sometimes involved the "scientific" predictions of Auguste Comte, and sometimes the "pleasant" ones of the Saint-Simonians, or sometimes the morphological ones of Marx, Michelet's phrase added the dimension of the dream. And it is easy to understand how Benjamin, so sensitive to the oneiric dimension of an epoch, could decide to include the oneiric prediction of Michelet in his Exposé.

Now, from Adorno's point of view, Michelet's phrase endangered nothing less than the very idea of the dialectical image; it placed it fundamentally in peril, by introducing a non-dialectic thematic: "All the themes of the theory of the dialectical image, and which seem to me fundamental to my critique, crystallize around this phrase, because it is undialectical." This is a crucial point, for Adorno will go on to say: "Eliminating this phrase will clarify the entire theory."[42]

42. Ibid., 171.

The thesis would be undialectical from three points of view:

First, the dialectical image would be reduced to a simple state of consciousness, as if the image were satisfied by recording the content of consciousness, even collective consciousness.

Secondly, the connection between the image and the future as utopia would be thought in a linear manner, even one whose course was predictable.

Thirdly, the era would be conceived of as a unified subject, that is, with no self-divisions, not riddled with contradictions.

In short, history would be thought of as a progression from the present to the future on the wings of the dream, a temporal process unrolling in a homogenous, contrast-free time.

In a certain sense, even if Adorno had not brought this up, the series epoch/dream/new epoch reproduces the schema of Karl Mannheim, of topos/utopia/new utopia.

Let us add that, returned to immanence via the evacuation of the theological dimension—the categories of salvation, of redemption—the dialectical image, disguised as being closest to social movement, would become non-dialectical, as if within the dream, the very idea of determined contradiction or negation were to become diluted.

2. Truly, in reading this letter, one might think Adorno was already accusing Walter Benjamin of "poetic empiricism." That is, that in order to be sensitive to symbolic expression, to the imaginary dimension of the socio-historical scene, Walter Benjamin was satisfied recording the contents of consciousness without making much of an effort to interpret or construct, as the dialectical image requires. And in fact the latter can only be constituted through an experience of contradiction, such that it contains within its very heart the engine of its own decline and renewal.

3. Now, this reproach of poetic empiricism, which would consist not only of merely collecting the immanent forms of consciousness, but more of "transposing the dialectical image as 'dream' into consciousness,"[43] would manifest itself at its most extreme with regard to the golden age, presented in unequivocal fashion in the Exposé.

43.
Ibid., 172.

The golden age, according to Adorno, who refers to Offenbach and certainly to the work of Kracauer on the latter, must be understood in a double sense, both as Arcadia and as hell, that is to say as the realm of subterranean powers, of myth and of terror. Reproaching Benjamin for having, additionally, abandoned the image of the nineteenth century as hell which, in this case, would distinguish it from utopia as dream, Adorno writes: "Now, this by itself [the image of hell] can put the image of the golden age in its proper place."[44] From this perspective, the golden age is to be henceforth conceived under the sign of ambiguity, its infernal possibilities contending with its Arcadian ones. Without this representation, we would end with a simplification of the golden age, and with a simplified analysis of the arcades' merchandise, with a radical separation between the golden age as a classless society, Arcadian, and the universe of commodity as purely and simply infernal. Just as we must proceed to a complicated vision of the golden age, seeing within it an infernal element, so we must complicate—and thus make more dialectical—our analysis of the realm of commodity. The latter, once it is constructed dialectically, is no longer simply infernal: for, by bringing its internal contradictions to light, we can see that it contains the possibility of going beyond this, that it is not a matter of simple regression to an anterior state of affairs. "To understand commodity as a dialectical image," Adorno writes, "means understanding it as the 'cause' of both its decline and its 'renewal.'"[45] Hence, to follow Adorno's critical approach,

44.
Ibid.

45.
Ibid., 174.

the interpreter cannot be satisfied with a simple collection of the dreams of the nineteenth century; he must, by means of a "dialectical construction," wrest the dream away from interiority, exteriorize it in order to appreciate to what extent it is part of the constellation of the real.

4. According to Adorno, by abandoning the necessary articulation between the golden age and hell, Walter Benjamin will have failed to see the complexity of the relationship between the Old and the New by conceiving it simply under the form of a "utopian reference to a society without classes."[46] Adorno sees this as non-dialectical to the extent that it figures in Benjamin's analysis as "an added, complementary element" and not "of the newest."[47] Benjamin, anxious to do justice to the research of Bachofen, would be guilty of having accepted, in an acritical manner, "the mytho-archaic category of the golden age" and thus of having opened the door, by means of a dualistic view of a two-strata utopia, to a mythic image to which he would remain prisoner, without having succeeded in transforming it so as to elaborate its true dialectical image. This would lead to the fear of falling back into "a massively mythical thinking," because when cut off from the image of hell, the theme of the classless society becomes subject to the tropism of myth: "The image of a classless society is antedated within myth, instead of appearing here in its transparency as an infernal phantasmagoria."[48]

To this warning Adorno adds a critique of the idea of the "collective" itself, considered as the subject of dream. Resorting to this subject would align Walter Benjamin, without his intending it, with Jung or Klages, having the effect of "hypostatizing archaic metaphors" and thus overvaluing them, provoking a blindness in the interpreter as to the possible source of dialectical images, which would no longer be "an archaic collective" but the individual, under the control of the bourgeois alienation typical of the age of commodity. "The collective consciousness," Adorno says, "was invented only to turn attention away from true objectivity and its correlate, that is, alienated subjectivity."[49] Adorno does not deny the existence

46.
Ibid., 173.

47.
Ibid.

48.
Ibid.

49.
Ibid., 173-74.

of interaction between the Old and the New, but in insistently linking the image of the golden age with that of hell, he keeps himself from perceiving in it a reassuring utopian reactivation of the classless society as if, to use an expression of Marx, one were to find "the most modern in the most ancient."[50] The decisive ambiguity of the golden age invites us to discern, behind this resurgence of images of desire in the nineteenth century, both what Benjamin himself called, in the "arcades book," the reactivation of mythic forces, a reactivation indivisible from the new sleep that capitalism engendered in Europe, as well as "the infernal phantasmagoria" that never ceased haunting the arcades, the attraction toward nothingness and toward death. This ambiguity clarified, Adorno says: "The category in which the archaic merges into the modern is less, it seems to me, that of the golden age than it is that of catastrophe."[51]

If we make this paradoxical vision of the golden age our own, it follows that the power of the archaic over the modern is no longer that of Arcadia but that of hell, the persistent rise of terror in the world.

Without claiming here to have considered Adorno's critique in its totality, let us nonetheless say that it seems particularly severe, not to say unjust, with regard to Benjamin. In fact, when we make our way through Benjamin's text, with the dualist interpretation of utopia he proposes, with those two strata, we could argue that in trying to complete Michelet, he has already broken with him. According to Michelet's phrase, each epoch carries within itself an orientation toward the succeeding one, and it is in the form of its dream—the image of desire, the oneiric image—that this orientation toward the future is manifested. In one sense, this oneiric image oriented toward the future would be that of modern *progressism* (that is, faith in progress) which, as we know, declares—whether with Saint-Simon, or with Fichte critiquing Rousseau—that the golden age is not behind us, but ahead of us.

Walter Benjamin, a critic of the modern conception of progress, adopts an original position, one that rejects the idea attributed to Rousseau as well as that of Fichte. The dream at work in each epoch will not be solely directed toward the

50.
Letter from Marx to Engels, 15 March 1868, cited by Löwy, in *Rédemption et utopie*, 150.

51.
Adorno in Benjamin, *Correspondance*, 173.

future, but will invent its relation with the near future by turning back toward the most distant past, the society with no classes, thus reanimating, motivated by a critique of the most recent past, "the land of Cockaigne, the ancient symbol of achieved desires." Thus, to the simplification of Michelet, with its single direction toward the future, Benjamin, aware of the complexity of symbolic expression, opposes the idea of the interpenetration of the Old and the New, as if this movement toward the new could only happen thanks to the revival of the image from the prehistoric past, that of the society without classes, as if the technology seized hold of a symbol already there, inherited, in order to renew it. He recognizes that the image of desire that constitutes utopia is mixed, composed not only of its own contents but also of its temporal orientation, since the orientation toward the future operates by means of a detour, a relation with the most ancient past.

This explains the link with the ancient symbol of the golden age, which perfectly circumscribes the space of critique for Adorno. He does not critique the orientation toward the past—insofar as it could be put into operation using a dialectical method—but rather the transfiguration of that past, so that the infernal element is hidden, with only the Arcadian element being retained. But might one say of Benjamin that, giving way to a crude realism, he inherits the symbol of the golden age as it was, without making it submit to any transformation, as if it were a matter of some positivity removed in history, or at the threshold of history, and it would suffice to rediscover it in order to retrieve it just as it was? Can anyone claim that Benjamin is ignorant of how the interpenetration of the Old and the New gives birth to fantastic forms?

Nor can one accuse Benjamin of simplification and "progressism" in the last section (VI) of the Exposé of 1935, "Haussmann or the Barricades," which comes to an end following critical work on the famous phrase of Michelet aimed at injecting dialectic into it, making it dialectical, to the extent that he puts every one of Michelet's terms to the test in order to substitute for an evolutionary schema a completely different picture. In fact, what is to be understood by epoch? How does the oneiric process function, and with what materials? Now, far from conceiving epoch as a unified or even harmonious whole, Benjamin perceives a crack in it, or somewhat more extreme, a "fissure," the onset of decline. Does this not open up another path leading toward the dialectical image? Citing Balzac, the first to evoke the ruins of the bourgeoisie, Benjamin observes that this fall, those ruins affect first "the symbols of aspirations from the previous century" before attacking the monuments of the dominant class. We see that the images of desire of the nineteenth century are always already in ruins, in pieces, the utopias as well as the arcades. And on that horizon of ruins appeared a new function of the dream: instead of being a plastered-over unity, so to speak, of the aspirations of the present epoch aiming at bringing about the succeeding epoch, the dream becomes a heterogeneous ensemble, made up of bits and pieces, as heterogeneous as the dreams of the individual. The materials that constitute it are no longer just "the residue of a world dream."[52] The dream is no longer the winged, aerial bearer of a painless transition into the future, to which one has only to abandon oneself, but it is instead, in the midst of that capitalism-engendered sleep, the presence of a universe that is both attractive and menacing— an infernal hodge-podge—in which fragmented images of desire are combined with mythic, archaic images from which the subject must tear himself if he ever wants to know awakening. To use an image dear to Benjamin, there is an arc reaching from sleep to awakening in the subject of the dream. Enough, then, of the representation that smiles and soothes to the point of numbness, and enough of the oneiric voyage toward the near future, of the gentle entry on smooth waters into the harbor of the future; let us substitute instead the idea, the necessity, the imperative of a difficult labor, with an uncertain outcome, in order to pull ourselves away from that state in which death prowls about, disguised behind various masks. Wakefulness, or nothingness. And thus Benjamin concludes his journey by reprising, but also by rectifying, the phrase of Michelet. Now, this displacement evidently escaped Adorno's critical observation, because in a sense the entire trajectory of

52. Benjamin, Exposé of 1935, Paris, 46.

Benjamin's 1935 Exposé consisted in crafting this essential rectification. "Every epoch, in fact, does not dream solely of the near future, but on the contrary seeks within its dream for a way to escape from sleep."[53]

53. Ibid.

Let us transpose Adorno's reading into analytical terms. If in analytical practice, it is not enough to simply catalog the patient's dreams or slips of the tongue, if instead they must be interpreted as symptoms in order to eventually give rise to the transformation of a neurotic structure, would anyone really consider that Walter Benjamin was in need of being recalled to vigilance?

Dialectical construction—and the dialectical image is the fruit of such a construction—proceeds in a manner like that of analytical practice, requiring interpretation, which is greatly facilitated by the ruin of nineteenth century symbols. The latter no longer impose themselves in their solidity, nor in their pseudo-positivity, surviving instead only in fragments, as residue, permitting interpretation's free play. Instead of passively recording or simply welcoming these "originary images," Walter Benjamin, aided by the destruction of what was real in the images, worked to disentangle the elements of mythic terror that the dreams carried within them, thus concluding his endless journey through the labyrinth of the arcades by exiting the world of sleep and coming to that of awakening. "Making use of the elements of the dream in the waking state," he wrote, "is the paradigm of dialectical thinking. This is why dialectical thinking is the organ of historical awakening."[54]

54. Ibid.

Moreover, to "rectify" the last part of Michelet's phrase: "Each epoch … seeks on the contrary to pull itself out of sleep"—does this not open up, in a way, the path to the interpretation of a problematic passage in the Exposé, one decisive for utopia, in section V, "Baudelaire, or the Streets of Paris"? This involves submitting the thesis about the duality of utopia to a new clarification, making it turn from being an empirical description—that of the two strata and their articulation—to having a philosophical meaning, one of ambiguity. It involves abandoning altogether the reassuring version of the two strata, with its realist tendency, from the prehistoric society without classes to think henceforth of utopia as caught between enchantment and disenchantment. Utopia, in the interpenetration of the Old and the New, would now be one expression among others of the ambiguity proper to modern capitalism: "the ambiguity that is proper to the productions and social relations of this epoch."[55] Thus, via the path of ambiguity, utopia will rejoin the ambiguity of commodity fetishism, and that of the arcades, which is the ambiguity of space, the arcade being at the same time glitter and poverty, the region of awakening desires and that of "complicity with nothingness." A double signification, neither superadded nor complementary, will mark utopia: the tension between the movement toward the New and the detour to the Old—the classless society of prehistory—this tension now redoubles, because this ancient symbol, the golden age or the Land of Cockaigne, is part Arcadia and part hell. The insistence on the idea of tension, instead of and in place of complementarity, sheds light on the relationship possible between utopia and dialectic. In fact, according to Benjamin, we can consider that "ambiguity is the manifested representation of dialectic, the law of dialectic at a standstill."[56]

Ambiguity, as the expression and perceptible manifestation of dialectic, can introduce a new image here—that of dialectic at a standstill—more complex than what we classically associate with the idea of dialectic. Indeed, dialectic is not only the deployment of internal contradictions and thus movement, but it can also be motionlessness, a standstill. This is in fact one of its birthplaces, and one of the definitions of the dialectical image. "When thought is immobilized in a constellation saturated with tensions, then the dialectical image appears."[57] To the dialectician, therefore, falls the task of constructing the dialectical image, that is, the space where the tension between dialectical contraries is strongest. Constructing a constellation saturated with tensions and immobile is not a moment of contemplative suspense, but the standstill of practice, and thus detachment from history—within the continuum of domination—in short, rescue. This ambiguity, this double signification reverses itself: instead of being a sign, the

55.
Ibid., 43.

56.
Ibid.

57.
Benjamin,
Paris, 494.

avowal of the weakness that afflicts utopia, it reveals itself as the fragile passageway between utopia and dialectic at a standstill.

"This standstill is utopia," Benjamin proclaims. This standstill of dialectic, insofar as it is rupture, detachment, rescue, is utopia in the sense of an upsurging of the New, arising out of a radical alterity. It is as if this immobilization of dialectic suddenly gave free rein to that escapism with which realist thought is constantly reproaching utopia, and to the whole category of escape, the no-place of utopia suddenly opening up the possibility of another, a different place. But one can also say inversely that utopia is a standstill, which is to say that utopia, instead of being a term to designate projection toward the future (the succeeding epoch), toward a better world as is commonly thought, constitutes itself in a standstill, takes its form within an immobilization: this is the moment of the construction of tensions, the explosion of contradictions rather than the emergence of a solution *hic et nunc*, an imperative rescue, a political choice. We might pause to appreciate the fecundity of Benjamin's idea, and its relevance to the libertarian utopia of William Morris, titled *News from Nowhere*, with its subtitle being *An Epoch of Rest*. This is the moment of standstill, this forgetting which is not reification, which allows the blossoming of utopia—or, to put it another way, utopia will never be constructed unless it is in a state of standstill, in a moment of suspension of the historical continuum—before the launch of another dialectic, impelled by a foreigner's visit, of forgetting and remembering, leading to a new awakening from the numbing that threatens the society that would be liberated. Out of this exchange between utopia and standstill arises the affirmation of Benjamin: "The dialectical image is thus a dream image."[58] This highly provocative declaration never ceases to be surprising. Can the dialectical image and the dream image be equated? Can we reduce the one to the other, without any further argument or proof? Is it true, to use Adorno's terms, that by transposing the dialectical image into consciousness under the form of the dream, Walter Benjamin has ended in a regrettable confusion? One interpretation of the arcades book takes special care to distinguish between the

58. Ibid.

two types of images. "A dream image is not yet a dialectical image, and desire is not yet consciousness."[59] What does this mean? Is this a matter of a veritable identification of the two, not to say a confusion? Would it not be better to recognize, on Benjamin's behalf, beginning with the ambiguity of the dreams of the collective but turning our attention toward the relationship thus unveiled between the dialectic at a standstill and utopia, that the dialectical image inscribes itself within the expressivity, whether symbolic or oneiric, of the nineteenth century, if only because it finds its support there, the ground from which it takes its flight? Up to a certain point, it belongs to the world of the dream—dialectical though it is, it remains an image—just as analytical interpretation belongs to the oneiric dimension whose reality it cannot ignore, even as it pulls back into the distancing and self-effacement of interpretation.

59.
S. Buck-Morss,
The Dialectics of Seeing,
114.

To appreciate this proposition in its fullest extent, we should measure the effect that arises from this encounter of the dialectical image and the dream, and we should determine in which direction the dialectical image pulls the dream image, in the shock of standstill that is utopia. If we think of it using the metaphor of lightning, the dialectical image is the energy that abruptly polarizes the field of the dream, pulls the dreamer up out of sleep, and pushes him or her toward awakening— or, to use a formula of Benjamin's from the arcades book, with regard to imminent awakening, the dialectical image *qua* dream image would be "the wooden horse of the Greeks inside the Troy of the dream."[60] The proposition that "the dialectical image is therefore a dream image" only takes on its full meaning when it is set beside this other idea that comes toward the end of the Exposé of 1935: "The exploitation of the dream elements in the state of wakefulness is the very paradigm of dialectical thought."[61] It is as if the moment of awakening, at the same time that it resolves the ambiguity of the dream images, or rather, clarifies them, dissolves the mythic-archaic aspect that had haunted them, thus detaching utopia from the enchantment that never ceased ruining it. When awakening rejects the mythic part that threatens utopia, it liberates the dialectical image within. But inversely, the dialectical image cannot do without the dream.

60.
Benjamin,
Paris, 409.

61.
Benjamin,
Exposé
of 1935,
Paris, 46.

After this discussion, which has amounted to a critical analysis of the famous Michelet phrase, can we continue to accuse Walter Benjamin of having remained below the level of dialectic, of being close at moments to Jung or Klages, of having proposed to us an idyllic image of the golden age while occluding its infernal side? Can we ignore the effort he has made to invite us to think utopia, "precipitated by the dream of the collective," under the sign of ambiguity?

In any case, in consulting the preparatory texts for the Exposé of 1935, it can be clearly demonstrated that Benjamin in no way ignored the relation between the golden age and hell. In plan 7, he wrote: "Dialectical schemata. Hell—golden age…. The golden age as catastrophe."[62] Thus the critique of Adorno, blind to some extent with regard to the critical work Benjamin had done, would be better viewed as a call to make more explicit what was still implicit, rather than a call for correcting some failure or doing away with some illusion. And this is how Benjamin understood it in his indirect response to Adorno—indirect in that it was addressed to Adorno's wife—where he expressed his agreement, in order to more clearly mark his resistance and surprise at his critic's lack of comprehension. In that letter to Gretel Adorno, of August 16, 1935, Benjamin begins by saying: "I omit a number of points in which I am in accord with you. (It is rare that I am so much in agreement with anything as I am with W's reflections on 'the golden age.')."[63]

Adorno's call is thus easily answered although, as we have emphasized, Benjamin had no need of his critique to become aware of the linkage between the golden age and hell. And thus he is far from purely and simply ceding to Adorno's criticisms. The letter's addressee could be witness to the partiality of his correspondent, dialectician that he is, having a tendency to confuse him with Jung or Klages, and failing to see the dialectical link between dream and awakening and the modifications made to the phrase of Michelet's, and also failing to have noted the relationship between standstill and utopia. Recalling a crucial problem for him, one that was at the heart of his project, Benjamin said: "As much as it seems pertinent for me to agree

62.
Benjamin,
Paris, 892.

63.
Benjamin,
*Correspondance,
1929-1940*,
185.

with W. in seeing the dialectical image as a 'constellation,' nevertheless it becomes all the more evident that certain elements of those constellations, noted by me, seem indisputable: these are the oneiric images. The dialectical image does not simply copy the dream: I have never wanted to affirm that. But it does seem to me to contain the instances, the sites where awakening occurs, and to produce its image only from these sites, as a heavenly constellation does with its points of light. Here therefore is a new bow that must be bent, a dialectic that must be mastered: that between the image and awakening."[64]

64.
Ibid., 186.

Thus, in his response Walter Benjamin most clearly defines his conception and role as sentry of dreams as taking hold of both ends of the chain so to speak —the image and the awakening—if one prefers that metaphor over the one of the bow. The image does not preclude the possibility of awakening, and inversely, awakening does not annul the existence of the image.

Contrary to Adorno, Benjamin recognizes an objectivity in the oneiric images. These oneiric images, not to be confused with the dialectical image, are inalienable. One cannot dismiss them by denying their existence—by reducing them to ideology, for example—nor by exchanging other images for them. At many points in the arcades book, Benjamin affirms the existence of the forms of the collective dream. In section K, "Cities of Dream and Houses of Dream, Dreams of the Future," after having asserted, as we have seen, the importance of the collective dream and its forms, Benjamin adds: "The collective expresses first of all the conditions of its life. The latter find their expression in the dream and their interpretation in awakening."[65] And again in *Experience and Poverty*: "They [men] have become exhausted and fatigued … after fatigue comes sleep, and it is not unusual for dreams to compensate for the sorrow and discouragement of waking life, and for them to depict life as fulfilled and even grand, though the power to make it so in waking life is missing."[66] Placing existence thus in a collective symbolic space, Benjamin keeps a firm grip on the existence and the consistency of these forms, despite their

65.
Benjamin,
Paris, 410.

66.
Benjamin,
*Expérience et
pauvreté*, trans.
J. Lacoste, 7.

ambiguity. And from this he draws his first thesis: these oneiric images are inalienable.

But again, to recognize the existence of these images in no way means that they occupy the totality of the scene and that one must end up confounding them, just because one has recognized them, with the dialectical image, as Adorno appears to believe when he accuses Benjamin of "transposing the dialectical image into consciousness under the form of the dream." Within the constellation that constitutes the dialectical image—that structured grouping of phenomena—one can no more ignore the oneiric image than one can "the sites of irrupting into awakening." If one were to schematize it as oneiric image + awakening = the dialectical image, one would understand Benjamin's barely concealed irritation as he continued to hammer the point: "The dialectical image does not simply copy the dream: I have never wanted to affirm that." Certainly, in the 1935 Exposé, he wrote, "The dialectical image is thus a dream image," but this formulation—a bold one, perhaps—only has meaning when taken as part of the whole arc sustaining it, going from image to awakening, and not frozen analytically in one of its moments, nor closed back in upon itself. It only takes on meaning when we put it together with the first part of the phrase signaling toward dialectic and toward awakening—"this standstill is utopia"—and with the transformation effected upon Michelet's phrase underlining how the dream, far from being a haven of peace and repose, can instead be considered as a site of conflict, of agon, with the dreaming collective itself trying, from inside the dream, to wrench themselves free into awakening. "The first sounds of awakening render sleep even deeper," Benjamin observes.[67] The dialectical image is thus a dream image affected by awakening, marked by, worked upon by the struggle to awaken.

67. Benjamin, Paris, 408.

Such is the narrow path opened up by Walter Benjamin, apparently not perceived by Adorno: neither negation of the dream image nor simple acceptance of it, not a simple recording but a *construction-interpretation* with its sights set on the emergence of the dialectical image and that of an awakening.

Also meriting consideration is Adorno's objection that the image under which the archaic slips into the modern would be less that of the golden age and more that of catastrophe. Certainly, to go along with Adorno, Benjamin would have been wrong to construct the relationship between the Old and the New as one of a utopian reference to a classless society. We can add that the power of the archaic in the form of catastrophe goes further, touches more profoundly the paradoxical vision of the golden age—Arcadia and hell—or even that along with the idea of hell, as Adorno conceives it, there is a specific consistency of the idea of catastrophe that cannot be reduced to the idea of hell. If hell can be an image of catastrophe, catastrophe cannot be reduced to hell. In *Negative Dialectics*, which has as one of its objectives to identify the blind spots in theory that are capable of having exercised disastrous effects upon the practice of emancipation, Adorno vigorously attacks the primacy of the economic in the theory of domination, whose origins he sees as coming from a certain Marxist quietism. Indeed, if domination comes only from the economic, the transformation of the latter, its abolition, must automatically and necessarily entail the end of domination: "The primacy of the economic must create, historically, and rigorously, a happy ending as immanent in the economic."[68] Noting, additionally, a certain presence of the *topos* of the golden age within the theory of Marx and Engels, Adorno concludes: "Their *imago* of the revolution constructs that of the primitive world."[69] Alerted by the failure of the revolution, of the revolution traduced in the twentieth century by the continuation of domination, Adorno opposes to Marxist theory the idea of the contingency of antagonism, or of an irrational catastrophe from the beginning, exterior to the economic, and close in a sense to the "unfortunate encounter" [*malencontre*] of La Boétie, and later, Pierre Clastres. His intent is not to affirm the perpetual nature of domination, but to strike a blow against the idea of universal history, to undermine the idea of a historic totality marked by economic determinism. "No universal history," Adorno writes, "draws a direct line from the savage to the civilized human, but there very probably is a direct line

68. Adorno, *Dialectique négative* (Paris: Payot, 1978), 251.

69. Ibid., 252.

leading from revolt to the atomic bomb."[70] We are invited to think of history under the sign of anxiety and, even more, to introduce the idea of catastrophe into our thinking of history, both in order to interpret history apart from a metaphysical quietism and in order to assign utopia, and those forces that struggle to rescue alterity, the role of resistance against total threat. On the one hand, Adorno says that "We must define the Spirit of the world, an object worthy of definition, as permanent catastrophe"; and on the other, he says that "Today, the aborted possibility of the Other is concentrated in that of avoiding catastrophe despite everything."[71] Adorno's objection is based on retaining what may be the intervention that impelled Benjamin to abandon the idea of the two strata in order to account for utopia and to effect a displacement that would consist not in moving from a paradoxical idea of the golden age to the idea of catastrophe, but in positing an equivalence between the two, the golden age as catastrophe—an equivalence not foreign to the ideas that Adorno developed in 1932 in the essay, "The Idea of Natural History."[72]

In any case, what was the effect to be of Adorno's critique in the letter of August 2, 1935? When we turn to the Exposé of 1939, can we say that the links to utopia have disappeared? Can we say that, faced with a sentry of dreams even more pitiless than himself, Walter Benjamin now located utopia entirely within the realm of myth? Or perhaps he continued to maintain a place for utopia while accepting Adorno's warning as to the ambiguity of the golden age, at once Arcadia and hell? Or, again, could it be that in taking on the idea of catastrophe formulated by Adorno, though not by him alone, Benjamin worked to displace utopia, that is, in profiting from the distance of the latter in relation to the dominant forms of thought and in relation to myth—an absolute distance, according to Fourier— Benjamin will now call on utopia to oppose catastrophe? Thus utopia will no longer be thought of as residing only on the side of oneiric images but also on the side of the energy that leads to awakening.

Walter Benjamin will invite us to develop a relationship with the *vis utopica* by orienting it toward the no-place of

70.
Ibid.,
250.

71.
Ibid., 250,
252.

72.
Adorno,
"L'Idée de
l'histoire-
nature," 15
July 1932,
trans. Philippe
Despois, in
*L'homme et la
société* 75-76
(Jan.-June
1985): 101-
116.

utopia such that, within the modern inversion of emancipation, the dialectic of emancipation, which reinforces the *continuum* of domination, utopia can create an irruption in history, opening up breaches in it. In short, to think utopia against catastrophe, we must see it as taking sides with the Copernican revolution that Benjamin was working to bring about in his book on the arcades.

THE EXPOSÉ OF 1939

In order to take into account the change in orientation we find in the Exposé of 1939, we can say that in that work, Benjamin opens up a passage from Michelet to Blanqui— that is to say, not so much a movement from progressivist republicanism to radical communism as one from a conception of history invoking progress (Michelet) to a conception of history under the sign of catastrophe (Blanqui)—or rather, drawing its energy and its heroism from the idea of catastrophe.

The effects of this change are immediately sensed: the section titled "Fourier, or the Arcades" is retained despite the negative advice Adorno had given, but the important paragraph from the 1935 Exposé that gave a general interpretation of utopia has disappeared, as if it were a matter of erasing a site of contention without actually—thanks to Fourier, in the name of Fourier—taking leave of utopia. This should not be a surprise, because a fundamental text from 1936 (note 1 of the French version of "The Work of Art in the Age of Its Technological Reproducibility") bears witness to Benjamin's permanent interest in utopia while at the same time it affords a glimpse of an attempt to give birth to a renewed interpretation, based on the opposition between the first and the second technologies.[73]

The first technology originates in the social ritual, in those magical practices within the group and in the service of the group whose aim is to set itself up in contrast to nature. "The first technology excluded the autonomous experience of the individual. Every magical experience was collective."[74] The first

73. I am indebted here to Bruno Tackels for his remarkable work, which has brought attention to the difference between the two technologies and has been able to show the importance of the subject with relation to the work of art and notably for the cinema: *Histoire d'aura: Benjamin, Brecht, Adorno, Heidegger*. Thesis presented for the doctorate in Philosophy, University of Strasbourg, 1994. See especially Chapter 3, "Benjamin et les deux techniques," 39-101.

74. Benjamin, *Écrits français*, 182.

difference is in the degree of investment: the first technology engages the person to the maximum extent, up to human sacrifice itself. "Once for all" is the motto of the first technology. We must note that the first technology is a process of producing the unique. While the first technology comprises a project of domination and mastery over nature, the second substitutes a distancing from nature, and play is its birthplace. "The origin of the second technology is to be found in the moment when, guided by an unconscious scheme, man learns for the first time to distance himself from nature. In other words: the second technology is born in play."[75] This distancing from nature, thanks to play, engenders a new relationship to it; instead of subjugating it, the second technology aims on the contrary to find "a harmony between nature and humanity."[76] Thus, we see a difference in tendency: the second technology engages the person as little as possible; the best analogy is with a remote-controlled airplane, with no pilot aboard. Its motto is "Once is nothing," which valorizes ever-renewed experimentation; its object is to go back over its experiences and choices while tirelessly varying and repeating them.[77] Finally, the second technology, separate from the will to subjugate nature for the benefit of the group, delivers the individual. "The first form of individual experience begins in play."[78] But far from envisaging history as a harmonious evolution from the first to the second technology, Benjamin instead conceives universal history as the theater of a battle, of a permanent competition between the two technologies, the first seeking to stifle play and its accompanying phenomenon, the appearance of the autonomous individual. Also, from this point of view, modernity, marked by the scheme of subjugating nature and imprisoning the individual, may be defined as the persistent ascendancy of the first over the second technology. Thus, within this conflicted modernity one may analyze revolutions as so many attempts to adapt the socio-economic structure of humanity to the development of the productive forces liberated by the second technology. Modern revolutions have it as their task to accelerate the process of adaptation.

75. Ibid., 148.

76. Ibid., 149.

77. "The second technology is the ensemble of the processes of (re)production of the multiple, while the first technology is a process of production of the unique. Its motto, 'once is nothing,' differentiates it from the first in giving an ever-growing place to the forms of play, an indefinite reproduction of the same." Tackels, 52.

78. Benjamin, *Écrits français*, 182.

With regard to this point, note 1 of the French version of "The Work of Art in the Age of Its Technological Reproducibility" sketches a new interpretation of utopia in relation to this reflection on modern revolution. As adaptation to the development of the productive forces of the second technology, revolution would be *innervation*: that is, it would tend toward constituting a new collective body of humanity (with no trace of organicism), giving to the latter new organs that would free it from the amorphous and heteronymous state of the masses. Revolution would make a new organ of the second technology for humanity. "Revolutions are the innervations of the collective element, or, more precisely, attempts at innervating the collective which, for the first time, finds its organs in the second technology."[79] And thus, conforming to the essence of the second technology, another attempt at the relationship with nature is born: instead of nature appearing as materials, as an exteriority that needs to be tamed, nature appears as an ensemble of forces with which it is possible to establish a "harmonious play." To go back to Fourier's terms, which are very much present in this note of Benjamin's, the second technology is what allows humanity to substitute for the "subversive" development of civilization (economic crises, wars, etc.) a "harmonic" one.

The acquisition of this new innervation, the reappropriation of the body, is conceived as similar to the infant's learning process. "Innervation, creator of the infantile gesture"[80]— learning to seize an object with the hand—does not signify, for all that, a precise appreciation of the object to be seized, nor of the distance to be traversed in getting hold of it. The act of seizing, in the learning process, in its very constitution, would be a kind of surplus with regard to the possibilities of grasping something. In the same way, historical innervation in the experience of the freedom that it discovers bursts through the boundaries of the possible. "And just as an infant learning to grasp extends his hand toward the moon as he would toward a ball within his reach, humanity, in its attempts at innervation, sees purely utopian goals as residing right next to achievable ones."[81] Revolution-innervation is the birthplace of utopia. In

79. Benjamin, *Écrits français*, ed. J-M Monnoyer 149n1.

80. Benjamin, cited in Tackels, 57.

81. Benjamin, *Écrits français*, 149n1.

that innervation, creator of humanity, utopia is anticipation in excess. The very particularity of the second technology can only serve to reinforce this tendency: in liberating the individual and his or her autonomous experience, it simultaneously places the individual into a "new field of play," overwhelming the field of possibilities, breaching the frontier between the possible and the impossible. As the individual takes the measure of the enslavement that the first technology exercises over him, he hurls himself "without measure" toward that new liberty and, just like the infant, he has no idea of the limits of this creative innervation. "It is precisely because this technology at first only aims at liberating the individual from the tasks that oppress him, that the individual suddenly sees his field of action expand immeasurably. Within that field, he does not know how to orient himself. But he already affirms his claims to it.... In short, it is the particular individual, emancipated by the destruction of the first technology, who lays claim to his rights."[82] In this new field of play revealed by the innervation of the second technology, the vital powers of the individual—which Benjamin identifies as the powers of love and of death— liberated from the destructive control of the first technology, now aspire "to impose themselves with a new vigor."[83]

Such would be the claim we must strive to identify in utopia, the key to reading the work of Fourier. In his conclusion to this extraordinary note, with regard to utopia and infancy, with regard to the relationship between utopia and revolution-innervation, Benjamin writes: "The work of Fourier constitutes one of the most important historical documents of this claim."[84] It might not be a complete betrayal of Benjamin's ideas to suggest that the Saint-Simonian doctrine, despite its project of world peace, tends toward the first technology with its watchwords about subjugating nature, while Fourier's utopia is clearly oriented toward the second technology and its emancipatory innervation.

It is no surprise then to find that the Exposé of 1939 focuses on Fourier's utopia in its uniqueness. And we should note that this analysis is preceded—not, perhaps, without irony— by an epigraph taken from *The Holy Family* by Marx and

82.
Benjamin, "L'oeuvre d'art . . ." in *Écrits français*, 149.

83.
Ibid.

84.
Benjamin, *Ecrits français*, 149n1.

Engels, to the effect that the first appearance of a mass interest in the public scene at the same time goes beyond its real limits. Thus it is not a matter of categorizing utopia in terms of an ahistorical Eden—the reference to the Land of Cockaigne has disappeared—but rather, to use the terms Marx used in *The 18th Brumaire*, ... to situate it among the "necessary illusions" that "exaggerate the task to be accomplished in the imagination," or "that magnify the struggles."

Utopia is thus reintroduced within a productive imaginary, and is far from being a sterile reference to some esoteric tradition. From this arises the generous reading of Fourier that Walter Benjamin would carry forward into his last text, "On the Concept of History."

Without mentioning its relationship to the second technology, Benjamin interprets the utopia of Fourier as finding its motive force in the appearance of machines; thus he analyzes it, with no negative connotation, as a machinery of the passions. Nevertheless, the "absolute distance" of Fourier is made clear, as within his utopia, play and harmony are associated together. "Fourierist harmony is the necessary product of this combinatory play."[85] Thus, this utopia envisages a movement beyond morality. Happiness is considered to be an effect, and the question is no longer to moralize or re-moralize humanity by an appeal to virtue, but to discover good mechanisms and good combinations such that the passions can express themselves in harmonious developments, rather than manifesting themselves in subversive ones. If this inversion of the mechanism of the passions had been realized then, "Nero would have become a more useful member of society than Fénelon."[86] With Marx's authority, Benjamin insists on "Fourier's colossal vision of man" that goes far beyond petit-bourgeois mediocrity and appeals to the beautiful soul. And finally Benjamin credits Fourier with distancing his project from man's exploitation of nature, as it reflects man's exploitation of man. Thanks to this distance, Fourier arrives at a vision of the possible reconciliation of technology and nature. "Technology appears as the spark that ignites the powder of nature."[87] At this level, though without being specifically mentioned, the opposition

85. Benjamin, Exposé of 1939, *Paris*, 49.

86. Ibid., 50.

87. Ibid.

between the two technologies re-emerges. The power of Fourier, perhaps, resides in his having abandoned the watchword of subjugating nature, which belongs to the first technology, in order to re-direct himself toward the "harmonious play" between technology and nature. We note how Benjamin insists on the "explosion of the phalanstery," to use Fourier's terms.

Clearly, even with regard to Fourier, the schema of the two strata has been abandoned: it is no longer a question of reactivating a golden age or signaling a classless society in prehistory. On the contrary, the evocation of a different relationship between technology and nature is faintly present already back in 1936, in note 1. Reading the notes in the arcades book, especially the extract labeled "J: Baudelaire," reminds us that Benjamin sees the greatness of Fourier in his having been the thinker who was able to create an image of the relationship between the creative innervation of the second technology and modern utopia. Indeed, was he not the one who had the audacity to situate utopia in the "space of play" cleared by the second technology, thus revealing the hidden relation between utopia and infancy? If the exploitation of human labor ceases, "labor will no longer be characterized by man's exploitation of nature. It will then follow the model of infantile play which, for Fourier, is the basis of the 'passionate labor' of the 'Harmonians.' One of Fourier's great merits is to have presented play as the paradigmatic image of labor that is no longer exploited. Such labor, in the spirit of play, no longer aims at the production of value, but rather at the enhancement of nature. Fourier proposes a model for nature too, one based on the play of children. This is the image of an earth upon which every region has become an 'inn' [*Wirtschaft*]. The double meaning of the word blossoms here: every region is worked by humans, who make every place useful and beautiful. But each one is open to all, like an inn by a road. An Earth cultivated according to this image would cease to be part of 'a world where action is never sister to dream.' The Earth would be a place where action is sister to dream."[88]

Given these conditions, it is easy to understand that Benjamin made the conjunction "Fourier, or the Arcades" into

88.
Benjamin,
"J: Baudelaire,"
Paris, 376-77.

a "point of resistance," to use Gershom Scholem's term, to save both the architecture and the meaning of the project, and that he had effectively resisted Adorno's counsel to drop this subtitle from the Exposé of 1935.

But for all that, one cannot affirm that the link between utopia and the golden age had disappeared in the 1939 Exposé. As in the Exposé of 1935, the section "Grandville, or the World Exhibition" presents a critique of the Saint-Simonian utopia, an industrial utopia on a planetary scale but one that is forgetful of the class struggle and thus blind to the question of the proletariat. Now, it is precisely under the sign of the golden age as enchantment that this critique unfolds. As in the 1935 version, the epigraph for this section is borrowed from a genuinely satiric piece from the era, *Louis-Bronze et le saint-simonien*, treating the theme of the golden age that is in our future, so dear to Saint-Simon and his disciples:

> Yes, when the whole world from Paris to China,
> Divine Saint-Simon, adheres to your doctrine,
> The golden age will be reborn in all its glory,
> Rivers turned to tea or chocolate,
> Sheep pre-roasted bounding on the plain,
> Steamed pike swimming down the Seine...[89]

89. Benjamin, Exposé of 1939, Paris, 50.

What are the world's fairs that transfigure or idealize the exchange value of commodities, according to a phantasmagoria involving a complex play between the specter of the golden age and the desires of the collective? Did these exhibitions play with the desire for the golden age in order to distract and divert the masses and, in so doing, contribute to their enslavement by turning them into a compact, heteronomous mass? In the 1939 Exposé, a link is revealed between the phantasmagoric traces of the golden age—within the framework of industrialized pleasure in the world exhibitions—and modernity as hell or, to use the phrase Benjamin used in his "First Notes," modernity "as the time of hell." The work of Grandville, which is correlate with the world's fairs, is it not torn between utopian and cynical elements—that is, between tendencies that reveal the false coin of the Saint-Simonian golden age of our future? "They [the world's fairs] thus give access to a phantasmagoria that a man enters into in order to be distracted. In the interior of these diversions that a man surrenders to, within the framework of the pleasure industry, he always remains just an element that is part of a compact mass. That mass takes delight in amusement parks with their roller coasters ... in an attitude of total reaction. The mass is thus led on to that state of subjection which propaganda, both industrial and political, relies upon."[90]

This perspective, which connects the image of the golden age with that of hell, becomes clearest in the deliberate care Benjamin takes in establishing a passage from Michelet to Blanqui. Let us recall the first effects of this deplacement: the elimination of the Michelet phrase, even though rectified, and the disappearance of the paragraph proposing a general interpretation of utopia. From this arises a new importance given to Blanqui, who goes on to play an exceptional role in the Exposé of 1939. He focuses the new project perfectly, figuring in the introduction and permeating the conclusion, from its epigraph to its closing line. Blanqui is substituted for Michelet, but this is the most secret Blanqui, the author of *L'Éternité par les astres*, written in 1872 at the Fort du Taureau prison, soon after the disaster of the Commune.

This permutation of names, of figures: does it reflect a response to Adorno's critique in the letter of August 2, 1935? Why connect Benjamin's reception of the critique, or call, of Adorno with the appearance of Blanqui? A hypothesis—and only a hypothesis: in order to respond to that interrogation. The movement from Michelet to Blanqui in the 1939 Exposé reveals that a kind of crystallization had come about between the objections of Adorno and the encounter with Blanqui, between the warning—the golden age must be thought of in its relationship to hell—and the infernal vision of Blanqui, as if Blanqui's very nickname, *l'Enfermé*, would quickly communicate an unexpected fullness of meaning to the Wiesengrund-Adorno objections.

90.
Ibid., 51.

In fact, during the years preceding the Exposé of 1939, Blanqui would up to a certain point play something of a teacher's role for Benjamin, or rather, that startling book of his, *L'Éternité par les astres*, would become a focal point for Benjamin's critical-cathartic work. For, if *l'Enfermé* had delivered a lesson, one that destroyed the mythology of progress (Benjamin saw him as treating it with derision), nonetheless he still did not escape the ambiguity of the nineteenth century, since in denouncing the phantasmagoria of repetition characteristic of modernity, in turn he went on to produce his own new phantasmagoria, thus nourishing the repetition of the phantasmagoric.[91] As Benjamin saw it, what happened was that, giving in to a nationalistic pattern of thought, Blanqui reproduced, as if in a prefiguration of the idea of eternal return, the dogmatic mythology that he denounced in the ideology of progress and perfectibility. "Blanqui's theory as a '*répétition du mythe*'—an essential example of the prehistory of the nineteenth century." The "eternal return" is the fundamental form of mythic, prehistoric consciousness. "It is a mythic consciousness because it does not reflect,"[92] says Benjamin, perceiving in the belief in progress and in the theory of the eternal return two complementary illusions, both of which must be rejected in order to achieve awakening.[93] "Belief in progress," Benjamin declares, "in an infinite perfectibility—an infinite ethical task—and the representation of the eternal return are complementary."[94]

These two moments are clearly perceptible in the Exposé of 1939. In the "Introduction," evoking the illusory security of nineteenth-century society, Benjamin introduces Blanqui as a kind of educator. "In that same period [that of the Commune], society's most feared adversary, Blanqui, revealed to it, in his last text, the terrifying aspects of this phantasmagoria. Humanity figures there as damned. Every new thing it could hope for turns out to be only a reality that has always been there; and the new will be just as incapable of providing it with a liberating solution as a new fashion is incapable of renovating society. The cosmic speculation of Blanqui teaches this lesson, that humanity will fall prey to mythic anguish as long as phantasmagoria continues to occupy a place there."[95]

91.
I refer the reader to my article, "Walter Benjamin entre mélancolie et révolution: Passages Blanqui," in *Walter Benjamin et Paris*, 219-247.

92.
Benjamin, *Paris*, 143.

93.
Ibid., 144.

94.
Ibid.

95.
Ibid., 47-48.

It is a teaching designed to encourage the salubrious winds of criticism to blow away the illusions of the nineteenth century, a teaching that calls for the destruction of all the phantasmagorias that surround and dominate it. The speculation of Blanqui denounces the phantasmagoria of modernity—or of modernity as phantasmagoria—as the nineteenth century proves to be the era of repetitions, not of newness—as if in the struggle between the Old and the New, the Old were to win out, but through the very experience of the New. This movement—which, to be more precise, is the negation of movement—engenders the return of myth which, wearing the mask of the New, reveals itself to be the terror and catastrophe of repetition. The "lesson of Blanqui" suggests the famous phrase of Benjamin's from the arcades book: "As long as there is a single beggar still around, there will continue to be myth,"[96] which invites the reader to consider the possible connections between beggary and phantasmagoria.

96.
Ibid., 417.

This is the teaching that dominates the rest of the section, "Fourier, or the Arcades": retaining utopia, and by doing so indicating that if utopia is to escape from modernity's phantasmagoria, we must work to sever it from myth.

But, regarding the second moment, the lesson of Blanqui must itself be submitted to critique, for this sworn enemy of illusions reveals himself to also be a fabricator of phantasmagoria. Opening the conclusion to his text titled *L'Éternité par les astres*, we read: "People of the nineteenth century, the hour of your apparitions is fixed forever, and it forever brings the same ones back to you." Benjamin notes the ambiguity of Blanqui, even as he recognizes the violence of his denunciation: "This book [*L'Éternité par les astres*] completes the century's constellation of phantasmagorias with one final phantasmagoria, a cosmic one."[97]

97.
Ibid., 58.

This reversal is ironic and tragic at the same time: Blanqui surrenders to the power that he denounces, the disenchanter finds himself re-enchanted. The idea of the eternal return that Blanqui conceives of with his cosmic thesis is at the same time "a terrifying indictment against society" and the crowning modern phantasmagoria. In fact, Blanqui's proposition—"that the New is always old and the old always new"—touches the very tissue of history, showing it to be, beneath its mask of progress, the phantasmagoria par excellence. "Here, Blanqui tries to trace an image of progress—antiquity immemorial parading itself as the latest, newest thing—that reveals itself to be the phantasmagoria of history itself."[98] And thus Benjamin stresses the extreme hallucinatory power of the texts and the feeling of oppression that overcomes the reader. To conclude the Exposé, he quotes almost in its entirety a page from *L'Éternité par les astres*, leaving aside two complementary themes of Blanqui—that of our nephews being assigned to a happier epoch than that of the nineteenth century, and that which asserts that whatever we could have been here on earth, we are somewhere else. It is as if Walter Benjamin had wanted to reinforce the impression of imprisonment, to put us even deeper into the prison of history and to block out even the tiny gleam of light that *l'Enfermé* allows us when he writes, "Only the chapter on bifurcations remains open to hope." The quotation from *L'Éternité par les astres* concludes with these damning words: "The universe repeats itself without end and paws the ground while staying in place. Eternity imperturbably plays out the same representations in infinity."[99]

Without a revolution that would be capable of giving birth to a new social order and undoing the enchantment afflicting the nineteenth century, the world is dominated by multiple phantasmagoria that endlessly repeat the struggle between Old and New, thus initiating a double movement, as much the repetition of catastrophe as the catastrophe of repetition. In this sense, Blanqui's vision is the phantasmagoria taken to its most extreme point, contaminating the very cosmos by projecting onto it the essence of modernity: a truly infernal vision. "Ultimately, novelty appeared to him like the attribute of everything that is damned. In the same way, in a vaudeville text written a little earlier, *Ciel et enfer*, the torments of hell are pictured as the very latest novelty of all time, as 'eternal and always new pains.' The men of the nineteenth century, who are addressed as if they were apparitions, come from this region."[100]

98. Ibid., 59.

99. Ibid..

100. Ibid.

In reading this new 1939 Exposé, the criticisms of Adorno seem to crumble away: Benjamin, far from seeing a reactivation of the classless society of prehistory in the impulses that give birth to utopia—but then, had this ever really been the case?—Benjamin, already animated by a suspicion of the golden age and on the alert for the infernal element it entails, can only view any connection between the oldest and the most modern with the greatest distrust, seeing in such a connection on the contrary the reactivation of the mythic powers most likely to bring on a renewed sleep.

Moreover, his reading of Blanqui, while accepting the violence of the critique, does not surrender to the hypnotic dogma of the eternal return—"the fundamental form of mythic consciousness"—and it clearly shows the justice of Adorno's remark that "the category under which the archaic slips into the modern is less that of the golden age than that of catastrophe." Benjamin's letter of January 1938 announces to Max Horkheimer "a rare find whose influence on my work will be decisive," that is, *L'Éternité par les astres*, and he already sees in Blanqui's text two elements that, as Adorno might have said, will aid in the perspective of "the arcades book," in understanding hell and the theological dimension. In that letter, Benjamin wrote: "If hell is a theological topic, this speculation may be defined as theological. The vision of the world that Blanqui sketches there borrows from mechanistic science, and it is in fact an infernal vision, but at the same time, in the form of a natural vision, it is the complement to a social order that, in the twilight of his life, Blanqui was forced to recognize as having defeated him."[101]

Seeing Blanqui as a spiritual brother to Baudelaire and Nietzsche, Benjamin underlined the ambiguity of this final text by *l'Enfermé*. "It represents an unconditional surrender, but at the same time the most terrible of accusations brought against a society that projects itself onto the heavens as an image of the cosmos."[102]

Thus, the displacement of Michelet in favor of Blanqui seems to be a response to Adorno's letter of August, 1935, a much stronger response in that it issues from the nineteenth century

101. Benjamin to Max Horkheimer, 6 January 1938, in *Correspondance, 1929-1940* II, 232.

102. Ibid.

itself, quasi-objectively, and from the pen of the man who incarnates the revolution in its most radical form. Not that Benjamin wishes to turn Blanqui into an authority. For having succumbed to the mythic powers that suffuse the representation of the eternal return, Blanqui ends in a "resignation without hope." And Benjamin with an equal vigor rejects belief in progress and the representation of the eternal return, "indissoluble antinomies" that, despite their differences, are united in opposing the dialectical concept of historical time.

After Benjamin's reading of *L'Éternité par les astres*, rather than becoming an authority for Benjamin, Blanqui becomes instead a new pole in the geography of Benjamin's thought, or rather an immovable column in the architecture of that thought, certainly an ambiguous figure, but one occupying a place symmetrical with those of Fourier or Paul Scheerbart. It is as if a new arc had been constructed linking the two figures, Blanqui/Fourier, or as if these two somehow precisely delimited the field of tensions marking the nineteenth century, as if the entirety of the field had to be rethought after considering Blanqui in opposition to Fourier, to the utopia of 1848.[103] Introducing Blanqui into the arcades project suddenly opens up a hitherto unexplored path, connections with Baudelaire and with Nietzsche. Such is the exceptional importance Benjamin grants to Blanqui in the Exposé of 1939, who in a sense dominates all its sections. In the overall structure of the work, the ideas in play on the side of Blanqui—the representation of the eternal return—are compared and contrasted with those in play on the side of Fourier or Scheerbart: the absolute break, the emergence of history as *continuum*, access to the radical New. At the extreme opposite point from Blanqui, with his hallucination of "a humanity living in a prison of immense size," and condemned always to return to the same, Scheerbart's novel, *Lesabendio*, presents us with "amiable and curious creatures" speaking an entirely new language, and rejecting any resemblance to the human.[104]

In order for this space to form a true field of tensions, he must keep his distance from the vision of Blanqui, while detaching it from the return of mythic consciousness that

103.
Benjamin,
Paris, 144.

104.
Benjamin,
Expérience et
pauvreté, trans.
J. Lacoste

dominates it, in order to transform what is presented as dogma, as ontology—being is repetition—into a proposition that has an "as if" value, into a hypothesis that, far from contributing to a closing down of the world, would, on the contrary, echo an urgent summoning to break open that closure, to bring the repetition to a standstill. It is only at this price that Blanqui can be of value as an educator, when the lesson he teaches succeeds in detaching humanity from "its mythic anguish" as opposed to plunging us back into it. And hence Benjamin's cunning in calling Blanqui to testify against Blanqui, to make the disenchanter stand up against the fabricator of the phantasmagorias that give in to the repetition of myth.

This new polarization does not bar the possibility of utopia, and neither does it deny its separate calling or its choice of alterity, but it does demand that utopia agrees to measure itself against its greatest antithesis—the idea of permanent catastrophe—rather than let itself be carried off on the peril-free waves of the golden age to come. Beyond the simple alternative, Arcadia or catastrophe, this new polarization of the field opens up a new, unexplored position for utopia, or rather, it imposes one upon it. Henceforth it must oppose that alternative, voice a refutation *hic et nunc*, even at the cost of keeping a vigilant eye on itself, knowing that the catastrophe that threatens it is, so to speak, an interior one, remaining ever on the alert so as to avoid myth slipping back in behind the mask of the *no-place*, so as to avoid a return to prehistory. This describes what it is to explore the field of tensions that Benjamin, the sentry of dreams, has constructed, this new challenge utopia must accept, the constellation of awakening to which it must direct us, if it does not want to discover with horror that utopian traits are actually Hippocratic ones, the traits of death. It is only by internalizing, making its own, the idea of permanent catastrophe, by accepting that trial, that it can preserve the chance of reaching another shore. "The concept of progress must be founded on the idea of catastrophe," writes Benjamin. It is the same with the practice of utopia. Exposed to the repetition of the same that haunts modernity, to the phantasmagorias that modernity supports, utopia can, under certain conditions, prove to be the place/ non-place of rupture with repetition, the place where the power of the evil spell dissipates.

The encounter with Blanqui is not the sort of thing that one forgets easily. The two-pole construction that results is carried forward in Benjamin's last text, "On the Concept of History."[105] Blanqui figures in Thesis XII, not under the sign of resignation, but rather as the incarnation of the revolution denouncing the reformism of the social-democrats. "In the course of three decades, they [the social-democrats] succeeded in suppressing the name of Blanqui, though that name had been the rallying cry that sounded throughout the preceding century." Hatred and the will to sacrifice would be the passions that would allow the current generation to honor the secret pact that had been concluded with past generations, and to implement the highly fragile messianic power that each new generation inherits (Thesis II).

Fourier is also present in Thesis XI. With no reference to the Land of Cockaigne, the author of *La Théorie des quatre mouvements* appears like nature's redeemer here. Opposite to social-democracy, which takes as its motto the subjugation of nature proper to the first technology, Fourier, as we see in note I of the French version of "The Work of Art in the Age of Its Technological Reproducibility" from 1936, is invoked and hailed as one who could respond to the productive powers born of the second technology, one who could imagine a new innervation of humanity such that a new space of play could be opened, one that could give free rein to a new harmony between humankind and nature. "The fantasies that have led to so much ridicule of Fourier now appear to be surprisingly sensible. Fourier thought that, thanks to a well-ordered social endeavor, we would one day see four moons illuminating our Earth's night, the ice retreating from the poles, sea water become potable, and wild beasts offer their services to humankind. All that illustrates a method of work that, far from exploiting nature, is capable of delivering creations from her womb that are only potential."[106]

105. Cited here from the French translation by Pierre Missac, which appeared for the first time in *Les Temps modernes* 25 (October 1947): 189-199.

106. Ibid., 195.

But beyond these explicit references to the two names, to the two poles, the movement of the "Concept of History" text sketches out the new task for utopia in averting catastrophe. In the encounter with the dialectic of emancipation—the process by which modern emancipation reverses or even inverts itself into its contrary—which is another sense of the term "catastrophe" and which manifests itself as the modern figure of repetition, utopia will be assigned the function, once the nodes of the dialectic are detected and isolated, of investing and orienting them differently, apart, we infer from Benjamin, from the ideas of progress, of the valorization of work and of the will to dominate nature. Thus, it becomes a matter of undoing the modern inversion of emancipation, and of opening the way to the excess that utopia carries with it, but even more, to keeping watch over the early utopian impulses so that the mythic repetition does not slip back in, does not sink everything back into an even deeper sleep, one that is cousin to nothingness, or one that, disguised as a departure or an escape, in fact effects a new imprisonment.

In order to achieve this change in function for utopia, or rather this change in orientation that will consist of disorienting utopia, the work of critique is not enough. Benjamin's arcades book is a call for a true transformation of utopia into the dialectical image that can be found everywhere in its pages.

Conclusion

What is the message we should hear in this appeal? Or rather, how can this metamorphosis of utopia into a dialectical image be brought about? From the beginning of the arcades project, the theme of awakening imposed itself on Walter Benjamin. In his view, it was precisely this emphasis on awakening that distinguished his project from that of the surrealists who, he thought, were all too inclined to allow themselves to slip into a new, hypnotic sleep. Benjamin tried, in fact, to walk a fine line, along a razor's edge in a sense: as he reaffirmed the unavoidable character of dream images, he also announced the necessity of metamorphosing them, that is, of finding an opening from which the mythic element could be extracted, to detach the oneiric material. What is there in utopia that is ready to perform metamorphoses, or how could utopia be made ready to do so?

Let us return to the idea of the dialectical image, which never ceases to be surprising. An image as such—is it not incompatible with contradiction, and thus does it not escape dialectic altogether? It is true that in the field of images, dialectic defines itself ambiguously. A dialectical image is first of all an ambiguous image, or rather one that has been ambiguous and one that at the moment of the standstill abruptly becomes dialectical. The standstill of the image, one could say. And at this moment of standstill, the ambiguity crystallizes and the contradiction blossoms, liberating the entirety of its emancipatory potency, almost as if the image were revolutionized. A double process is at work, both destructive and liberating, a dazzling process that Benjamin compared to atomic fission. And thus it is through its ambiguity that Fourier's utopia is brought to its metamorphosis: it contains, on the one hand, a *Biedermeier* or Modern style, but on the other it also has a ludic side, a space for play that reflects the second technology and the possibility of a harmonious relationship with nature. At that moment of danger, in the face of the catastrophe that was returning to his present—fascism, the totalitarian State, the reign of the first technology with its motto of subjugating nature—it was a matter of taking possession of Fourier's utopia, of bringing about its blossoming in order to dissolve its ambiguity and to liberate its rescuing power as well as its truth content. Is this not the work Benjamin had dedicated himself to in "On the Concept of History" with regard to Fourier? In that sense utopia, as the dialectical image, is distinguished from the concrete utopia of Ernst Bloch, who denies the distance there is at the outset between the utopian approach and dialectics. "At the moment of danger": this precision can help us advance in our understanding of the process and of what would make it possible, help us enter into "the Copernican revolution," to use Benjamin's metaphor. For it is in the course of a Copernican revolution that utopia, a dream image under the control of myth, can suddenly become a dialectical image. At this point we may turn to Marie-Cécile Dufour El Maleh and her patiently elaborated work, which suggests the guiding thread running through the extensive Benjamin canon. "It now seems evident that the life and the writings of Walter Benjamin are entirely oriented toward allegory [l'écriture-allégorie] or rather that they emanate allegory themselves. Salvific allegory is the place from which his work always originates."[1] She also points out the allegorical gesture—reading one book in the light of another one—that permitted Benjamin to implement his cathartic critique of utopias. Allegory diverts the archaic images and the myths that nourish them; linked to the "destroyer character," allegory creates a new arc leading from, at one end, the recognition of images from the collective dream, to, at the other, the necessity of exposing those images in order to glean from them, in their ruin, beneath their ashes, the spark capable of opening up an unsuspected pathway. In short, the sentry of dreams is by necessity an allegorist.

What are we to understand by this "Copernican revolution" phrase? What did Walter Benjamin want to signify by adopting this phrase of Kant's? The awakening, whether conceived in individual terms or in terms of a generation, can be conceived

1.
Marie-Cécile
Dufour-El
Maleh,
L'Écriture
allégorique (La
Pensée
Sauvage,
1999), 85.
By the same
author, see
Angelus Novus
(Brussels:
Ousia, 1990),
and La Nuit
sauvée
(Brussels:
Ousia, 1993).

as a gradual process. Pursuing the comparison, Benjamin says that sleep is the first stage for generations, and the experience of the dream is the experience of a generation's youth. While previous generations can rely on general tradition for interpreting their dreams, the present generation, which has lost "all the natural and physical resources of dream recall," is in this respect entirely deprived. Thus Benjamin attempts to develop "an essay on the technology of awakening," and this is clearly the object of his Copernican revolution in his vision of history. In the past, Yesteryear constituted a fixed point, and the present revolved around that point in order to acquire, "on tiptoes," the best knowledge possible. For someone involved in the Copernican revolution, the present now becomes the fixed point around which Yesteryear orbits, so that now, with "a tiger's leap," the present takes hold of Yesteryear, immobilizing it (fixing it), and forcing it to reveal its contradictions and dissolving its ambiguity (dialectical fixing). The dialectic of the standstill: "The immobilization of thoughts," Benjamin declares, "is part of thinking, just as is their movement. When thought comes to a standstill saturated with tensions, then appears the dialectical image. It is a caesura in the movement of thought."[2] In this complex movement of brutal rupture, awakening can be effected, snatching the dreamer from that hypnotic sleep that keeps him in close proximity to death. The dialectic specific to dream recall, oriented toward Yesteryear, is the tiger leap, because it is oriented toward emancipation, and it keeps a sharp eye out for the tiny fault line from which a fragile chance of liberty might issue, and grabbing hold of it, it seeks escape from the repetition of catastrophe. A dialectical reversal commences. According to the exigencies of the present, it is necessary to constitute Yesteryear, to construct a new configuration through mediation and through recall ("remaking Yesteryear in the memory of the dream") and thus to awaken; the awakening and dream recall are closely related. For Benjamin, then, is awakening simply an exemplary form of dream recall? Not to accept Yesteryear like a given already there, which one can inherit like a bequest, but instead once constructed, once polarized, to make it blossom so as to

2. Benjamin, *Paris*, 494. See also this other definition, from 479: "An image, on the other hand, is that wherein Yesteryear encounters Now in a flash, forming a constellation. In other words: image is dialectics at a standstill."

liberate its emancipatory powers, in order to effect the rescue of what threatens to be lost. Benjamin specifies that "the dialectical image is a lightning-like [*fulgurant*] image. Thus, an image flashing forth in the Now of knowability is what must be seized in order to hold on to Yesteryear. The rescue that is effected in this way—and only in this way—can only ever be accomplished with what will be lost without hope of salvation for the sake of the next."[3] The dialectical reminder of past circumstances, Benjamin explains, "lights the fuse of the explosive that lies buried in Yesteryear."[4] The technology of awakening, thanks to which the world of one who dreams is transformed into a world of wakefulness, a world of vigilance, one that does not shirk from answering the call to rescue. Awakening is indeed the Copernican revolution in act, the dialectic of the dream recall. Benjamin's goal in his arcades book thus redefined and made explicit (that is, the elaboration of an unknown technology of awakening): how can we fail to see in "On the Concept of History" this Copernican revolution being implemented at the moment of danger? Far from devoting himself to an academic work with, among other goals, the aim of writing a critique of Hegel's philosophy of history, Benjamin instead gives himself over to an intensely concentrated spiritual exercise, working to produce dialectical images capable of awakening the collective dreamer sunk in a half sleep, to pull away the leaden weight that so heavily bows down the destinies of his contemporaries. At the moment of extreme danger, if we invoke Blanqui, what will he say to us? If the revolutionary impulse is born out of indignation over the reigning injustice, might Blanqui's concept of catastrophe, rather than leading us toward an abdication of responsibility, instead provoke in us the obligation "to detach humanity at the last second from the catastrophe that threatens it every time"? Reconstructed in this way, the image of Blanqui might re-emerge from beyond the ambiguity afflicting it: instead of diffusing the mythic narcotic of the eternal return of the same, it might function as a stimulus to awaken.

The Copernican revolution thus redoubles. The work of Walter Benjamin no longer responds to a desire to know (to

3. Benjamin, *Paris*, 491.

4. Benjamin, *Paris*, 409. The Copernican revolution is primarily defined on 405 ff., and on 880-81.

know the historical object that would be Yesteryear, as best as possible), but instead it obeys a political imperative, to allow the present to be born, and it responds to the urgency of the present, to the summons that gives the sentry the eyesight of a lynx, so that he can clearly discern within Yesteryear the point of intervention, the point where the shell can be broken, where the rescue can begin. "Approaching the past," Benjamin declares, "means that we should study it not the way we used to, in the manner of the historian, but in a political manner, using political categories."[5]

Utopia accompanied Benjamin throughout his life. We know, from the work of Jacob Taubes, that Benjamin wrote an account, unfortunately lost, of Ernst Bloch's *The Spirit of Utopia*, after its first publication.[6] Pierre Klossowski, who knew Benjamin well during the last years of his life, recalled in 1969 that deep down, Benjamin "held onto a personal version of a phalansterian renewal. Sometimes he would talk to us about an 'esotericism' both 'erotic and artisanal' that underlay his explicitly Marxist conceptions. Sharing the means of production would allow society to substitute for the now abolished social classes a redistribution into *affective classes*. An emancipated industrial production—instead of subjugating affectivity—would cause its forms to flourish, and in organizing its exchanges would turn work into the accomplice of powerful desires, ceasing to be the punitive payment for them."[7]

5.
Benjamin, *Paris*, 409.

6.
Jacob Taubes, *La Théologie politique de Paul* (Paris: Seuil, 1999), 108.

7.
Pierre Klossowski, "Entre Marx et Fourier," in *Le Monde*, 31 May 1969, supplement #7582 (a special page dedicated to Walter Benjamin). See also Denis Hollier, *Le Collège de sociologie, 1937-1939* (Paris: Gallimard, 1995), 883-885.

* * *

A sentry of dreams in the manner of Walter Benjamin? He was one who never rested from the struggle of detaching utopia from myth, one whose vigilance detected the tiny fault line, the breach into which one could rush in order to pull the sleeper up and let him know wakefulness. The sentry of dreams also became a pearl diver, leaving this maxim deposited with us: whenever we have the word "utopia" on our lips, the imperative to rescue it will always be present.

Univocal Publishing
411 N. Washington Ave, Suite 10
Minneapolis, MN 55401
www.univocalpublishing.com

ISBN 9781945414008

Jason Wagner, Drew S. Burk
(Editors)
All materials were printed and bound
in November-December 2016 at Univocal's atelier
in Minneapolis, USA

Publisher: Jason Wagner
Director: Drew S. Burk
Production Manager: Gina Newman
Design Assistant: Geoffrey Anderson
Editorial Assistant: Lia Swope Mitchell

This work was composed in Centaur & Universe
The paper is Hammermill 98
The letterpress cover was printed
on Crane's Lettra Fluorescent
Both are archival quality and acid-free